The Self-Catering Holiday Guide to Shopping and Cooking in Europe

The Self-Catering Holiday Guide to Shopping and Cooking in Europe

Nicholas Courtney

Illustrated by Val Biro

Hutchinson

London Melbourne Sydney Auckland Johannesburg

Hutchinson & Co. (Publishers) Ltd

An imprint of the Hutchinson Publishing Group

3 Fitzroy Square, London W1P 6JD

Hutchinson Group (Australia) Pty Ltd
30–32 Cremorne Street, Richmond South, Victoria 3121
PO Box 151, Broadway, New South Wales 2007

Hutchinson Group (NZ) Ltd
32–34 View Road, PO Box 40–086, Glenfield, Auckland 10

Hutchinson Group (SA) (Pty) Ltd
PO Box 337, Bergvlei 2012, South Africa

First published 1980

© Nicholas Courtney 1980
Illustrations © Hutchinson & Co. (Publishers) Ltd 1980

Set in VIP Baskerville

Printed and bound in Great Britain by
Fakenham Press Limited, Fakenham, Norfolk

British Library Cataloguing in Publication Data

Courtney, Nicholas
  The self-catering holiday guide to shopping and
  cooking in Europe.
  1. Marketing (Home economics) – Europe –
  Handbooks, manuals, etc.
  2. Cookery, European
  641.3   TX356

ISBN 0 09 140850 4 cased
     0 09 140851 2 paper

Contents

Acknowledgements

I would like to thank the dozens of shopkeepers and stall-holders throughout Europe who, forsaking queues of customers, gave me such invaluable help with this book, as did Food from France in London and Paris, José Letona Director of the Spanish National Tourist Office in London, Salvador Amoros Dupuy in Madrid, J. J. Castillo, Eduarda de Olivera of the Portuguese Tourist Office in London and Teresa Gameiro das Neves in Lisbon, Roberto Branco of the Sol e Mar Restaurant in London, Juiliana Berteletti of the Italian State Tourist Office in Rome, Marquesa Marita Guglielmi and her amazing chef, Armando, and Marquese Edoardo Talamo, Jane Rivaz and Mrs Mary Antonopoulou of the Greek National Tourist Office and the girls in Villa Venture. Vanessa Hardwicke and Elizabeth Paget typed superbly. Alwyn Wheeler of the Natural History Museum kindly checked the fish sections.

And most of all I thank Vanessa, to whom this book is dedicated.

Introduction

More and more people are cooking for themselves on holiday in villas and apartments, caravans, tents, or on boats. Many more would like to escape the 'little England' atmosphere and food of the foreign holiday resorts but are put off by the prospect of shopping in another country and the difficulties of cooking unfamiliar produce.

This book shows how to shop in France, Spain, Portugal, Italy and Greece: and once all that excitingly new and different food has been recognized and bought, the recipes tell how to cook it in local style. To some the sections on wines and spirits will be of greater importance; but whatever your tastes, or your experience of cooking for yourself on holiday, this book will have something of value.

To experience a market day in a small village anywhere on the continent, with its colourful array of striped awnings, stalls piled high with the freshest vegetables and exotic fruits, and fish of every colour, size and shape, is to become a part of the bustling life of the village. There is even something special about a supermarket abroad!

As well as the attraction of the colour and atmosphere of the market, local produce in season can be very cheap. Imagine the joy of finding vegetables such as artichokes, egg plants or peppers (so expensive in the United Kingdom!) plentiful and inexpensive; choice, delicate fruits such as peaches practically given away in boxes, lemons by the sackful – or melons, ripe and delicious, sold for the equivalent of a few pence.

Holidays are a time for exploring. There are so many new things to try: the dozens of Mediterranean fish (even the common sardine or anchovy takes on a new taste when absolutely fresh); those succulent loquats or medlars and prickly pears sold by the roadside; strange-looking celeriacs and salsify. Each country has its own surprises and its own special way of preparing them.

The book is divided into five main chapters – on France, Spain, Portugal, Italy and Greece – and each chapter split in two – a shopping section and a cooking section. The shopping section lists the various shops and market stalls, explaining what they sell. Drawings (not to scale) or descriptions help you recognize some of the more unusual produce and unfamiliar Mediterranean fish, and also how they are sold – straight kilos, by the piece or in strange *etti* or *oaks*!

One of the special delights of eating on the continent is the tremendous variety in the styles of cooking, not only between the countries but between the regions as well. However, even though everyone likes to eat and drink well no one, particularly on holiday, wants to spend hours preparing a meal: so the recipes have been chosen with great care. They are quick and simple to prepare, making the most of the local produce in season and are all typical of their country of origin or of their region. With a very few exceptions each recipe can be prepared in any of the five countries – so if you do not find a recipe in France for, say, angler fish, the index will tell you that the Spanish have an excellent one that can easily be used in France.

More emphasis has been placed on fish, fruit and vegetables than on meat, as they are much cheaper and more readily available; and as there are so many summer fruits, delicious ice creams and tempting cakes and pastries, as well as cheese, sold everywhere, only a few choice recipes for sweets have been included.

Where possible, plan your menus for one day – two if a weekend or a saint's day – that way everything will be as fresh as possible and there should be little wastage. The traditional opening times of the shops cater for those locals without fridges who have to market for each meal.

Even a cursory glance through this book tells you that you will miss out on one of the delights of your holiday – the shopping – if you arrive laden with food from home. There are, however, a few items that are so much cheaper in Britain they are worth taking; butter, instant coffee (transfer it to a plastic bag if you are flying), packet bacon (eat it quickly!), tea or tea bags, marmalade, chocolate and Marmite (if you cannot do without it). Powdered milk is useful, particularly in Spain and Greece, and aluminium foil, 'Clingfilm' and those pull-off plastic bags are invaluable and sometimes hard to come by abroad.

For the rest, make the most of the local delights and have a wonderful holiday.

A WORD ON THE RECIPES

I have tried to keep the recipes as simple as possible, so you won't find here those classic recipes that demand hours of intricate preparation in a really well-equipped kitchen. Instead I have chosen dishes that are typical of their countries, yet are easy to make and use generally cheap and easily available ingredients. Many of them are commonly cooked at home, yet never find their way on to restaurant menus. I have also left out dishes which are better eaten out rather than made yourself: Italian *pizza*, for instance, can be made at home and cooked in an ordinary oven, but it tastes better made in quantity and cooked in an enormous special *pizza* oven – and it is almost as cheap bought at the *pizzeria* as it is cooked at home.

Oven temperatures are never absolutely critical, so you can adjust cooking times to suit the vagaries of an unfamiliar oven. Whatever the markings in Centigrade or numbers on the dial say, oven temperatures basically fall into the three categories, slow, moderate or hot – and these are used in the book. Many of the slow-cooked dishes can be cooked on top of the stove if you don't have an oven.

Here are a few helpful equivalents:

A wineglass is 5 fluid ounces, 150 millilitres or $\frac{1}{4}$ pint.
A tablespoon is $\frac{5}{8}$ fluid ounce or 18 millilitres.
A pint is 4 wineglassfuls or 600 millilitres.
A litre is $1\frac{3}{4}$ pints.
A kilogram (1000 grams) is $2\frac{1}{4}$ lb.
500 grams is a little over 1 lb.
100 grams is about $3\frac{1}{2}$ ounces.

Metric quantities are given first in the recipes, as you will have bought metric amounts when shopping.

Continental cooking relies heavily on oil. Butter is used in northern France and northern Italy, but otherwise oil is used where we often use butter, margarine or dripping as it is cheaper and much easier to store. The best is olive oil, which comes in various grades and prices. First-grade oil is usually worth the extra cost, as second- and third-grade is much lower quality. The colour is a guide. Clear, yellowish oil is purer. Darker oil tending to a green colour is less pure and tastes stronger, more like the olive fruit; if you like strong-tasting oil, this is the one to buy. Always use olive oil for mayonnaise and salad dressings; for frying, etc. a cheaper oil will do – you can always improve its taste by adding a little strong olive oil for the flavour.

A few sauces and dressings are common to all the countries and indispensable for cooked dishes and salads. They are on pages 203–4.

Where tomatoes are cooked – and that is in many recipes – you may want to peel them first. Pour boiling water over them and leave them for a minute or two. Then the skins will split and remove easily. It is much easier to leave the skins on, if you don't mind finding the bits in the cooked dish; when it is essential to skin tomatoes the recipe says so.

Crushed garlic is needed in some recipes. A good tip is to crush the clove with a little salt against the back of a wooden spoon.

A WORD ON BARBECUING

There can be no better way to cook your food than on an open grill or barbecue. Many villas will have one already built, but if you do not have one already, a few stones with a grille, or strong wire netting will do. In Portugal, the home of the grilled sardine, they have a special cast-iron brazier called a *fogareiro*. In France, Italy and Greece they like to grill over old vine cuttings or olive wood to give the food added flavour. Whatever wood you use, make sure that it has burnt right down so that you are cooking on glowing embers and not flames and smoke!

Barbecuing fish

Before you start it is useful to make up a mixture of olive oil, a little lemon juice, a small leaf herb like oregano, thyme or *rigani*, and salt and pepper. Mix these in a bottle with a screw top pierced with small holes to make a shaker.

Scrape off the scales with a sharp knife and wash. For larger fish make slanting cuts down the body on both sides, then insert slices of lemon, tomato or onion.

Paint the bars of the grill and the fish with the olive oil mixture. Place fish on the grill, occasionally sprinkling with a little more of the olive oil mixture. (Avoid spilling the oil on the embers as this makes them flame and burns the fish.)

The fish should need turning only once. It is cooked when the flesh is white to the bone and comes away easily.

Most fish is suitable for grilling. Sardines, red mullet, mackerel, sea bass, sea bream, trout, grey mullet and hake are best. Slices or steaks of larger fish like swordfish are also good, and grilled prawns are excellent.

Barbecuing meat

Any lean, not-too-thick cuts of meat, trimmed lamb or pork chops, chicken, quail and kidneys are all excellent grilled on a barbecue. The meat is better if marinated for about an hour in a mixture of equal quantities of olive oil and white wine, seasoned with a small leaf herb like oregano, thyme or *rigani*, salt and pepper and a squeeze of lemon juice. Paint the bars of the grill with some of the marinade and cook the meat gently, turning once. The better cuts of meat take about 10 minutes on each side to cook, but allow a little longer for chops, sausages and chicken.

A WORD ON BUYING FISH AND SHELLFISH

All fish sold on the continent is likely to be absolutely fresh, but there can be disastrous exceptions and bad fish, especially shellfish, can have dire consequences – nothing less than that sure holiday-stopper, food poisoning.

To be absolutely safe here are a few pointers: the eyes should be bright and proud, the gills bright red (except for mackerel), the flesh firm and elastic (check by poking it with your finger – the dent should immediately spring out). The scales should be bright and stick to the fish and not the slab, and there should be no smell, other than a vague tang of the sea.

And, after taking trouble to buy fresh fish, always cook it and eat it the same day.

Tired fish can be enlivened by washing in salty water with some lemon juice. Fish will not keep long in a hot kitchen. It should be kept in a cool place or in the refrigerator, lightly salted and covered with a damp cloth. Shellfish is absolutely safe to eat so long as you are careful: mussels, clams and cockles must be alive right up to the point when they are cooked. You can check by tapping the open shells with your finger: if they do not close, or if the shell is broken, they must be thrown away. Likewise if they do not open when they are cooked, they are bad. Live cockles very often have a 'foot' hanging from the shell. Most likely, shellfish will be sandy inside, and a good way of 'purging' them is to put them in a bucket of salted water overnight and feed them with a little crumbled bread. As the mussels or clams open to feed they drop out the sand and grit. The king of the shellfish, the oyster, if taken raw should always be eaten alive. In the Mediterranean it is probably better to cook the wild varieties.

Many people are put off by the look of octopus, squid and cuttlefish – all that white slimy flesh and those tentacles! This is a mistake, as they are cheap and delicious. In most places they will have been prepared ready for cooking. If not, ask the fishmonger to do it for you, or at least to show you how to do it. If you are left with a squid to prepare just follow these simple directions: grasp the head section in one hand, the fin and body in the other and pull apart gently. Very carefully remove the ink sac and keep. Cut the tentacles from the head just above the eyes and pick out the small round 'bone', then pull out the pen-shaped transparent cartilage from the body. In plenty of cold water rub off the inky outer membrane and wash the insides thoroughly.

Cleaning an octopus is very similar. Simply cut off the eyes and remove the 'beak', a transparent 'bone' behind the eyes, and the ink sac in the body. Wash the grey slime off the body in plenty of cold water, then either flay the octopus with a stick or beat it on a rock – tentacles and body – until it is tender. It is really worth the trouble even though you may not think so at the time!

A WORD ON WINE

In all these countries, there is little or no duty on wine, so it is startlingly cheap by British standards.

The cheapest wines generally come in plastic or returnable glass bottles with plastic or metal tops; they tend to be vague about their origins, and just tell you the brand name and a phrase like *vin de table* or *vino da tavola* ('table wine'). Most taste very rough, until you get used to them.

At the other end of the scale, expensive wines are much the same price as in Britain, because duty, even at British levels, makes up only a small proportion of the British price.

The best value for money is in the middle of the range: the wines which are much better and a little more expensive than *vin ordinaire*. Everywhere you will find local wines. Most of them don't travel far – so catch them when you can. Some are marvellous, some are awful, so if you don't like one try others.

The top of this middle range is mostly covered by the *appellation* system which guarantees quality (except in Greece). Look for the words on the label: *Appellation controlée, A C* (France); *Denominazione di origine controllata, D O C* (Italy), *Denominación de Origen, D E O* (Spain); *Denominacão de Origem, D E O* (Portugal). There is a second level of *appellation*, below *A C*, called in France *Vins délimités de qualité supérieur, V D Q S*, in Portugal *Reserva*, in Greece *Eidikos diatirimenon* (Ειδικως διατιρημμιενων) these wines are always good and appreciably cheaper than *A C*.

Whether it is cheap or expensive, wine doesn't keep well once the bottle is opened. You can (just) open a bottle at lunch-time and finish it in the evening, but don't try to keep a bottle half-full overnight.

A glass or so of wine in the cooking helps the flavour of most savoury stews and cooked sauces.

When you are really thirsty, try the continental habit of drinking wine mixed half and half with water.

France

SHOPPING

Shopping in France is a joy – for who can resist those endless delights from the *charcuterie*, the pastries filled with fresh cream or fruit, or the tomatoes in the market still warm from the sun? Who can ignore the fishmonger's slab, with its confusion of fish of every shape, size and colour – silver and grey, rose-pink and blue-black? And who can pass by the fresh green salads and the full ripe sweet peppers, or the lean flesh of red beef tied ready for roasting?

Market day in France is a special day even though it takes place three times a week in the large towns, twice in the smaller towns and once a week in the more important villages. It is a hive of activity from the moment the first traders arrive around 6 a.m. to set up their stalls and unfurl their striped umbrellas ready for the early shoppers, right up to mid-day when they hope to have sold out completely. The cities and important towns have covered municipal markets but again, except in Paris, they trade only three times a week.

The working day in France starts early and most shops, such as the butcher *boucherie*, fishmonger *poissonnerie*, the delicatessen *charcuterie*, the greengrocer *marchand de légumes*, and the grocer *épicerie*, are open at 8 o'clock. They close for lunch between half past 1 and 3 o'clock, finally packing up at 8 o'clock at night. The baker's shop *boulangerie*, usually part of a pastry shop *pâtisserie*, opens even earlier to sell the still-warm bread, *croissants* and *brioches* for breakfast. They stay open (usually with a 2-hour lunch break from 12 till 2) until 8 o'clock.

The supermarket *le supermarché* acts independently of the rest of the town, simply opening at half-past 8, closing for lunch at 12.30 and opening in the afternoon between 2 o'clock and 8, sometimes between 2 and 10 in the larger towns.

Fermé le lundi means 'closed on Mondays'. All through France shops close on Mondays – some just in the morning, others (like butchers and fishmongers) all day. Very often they close for another afternoon in the week or on Saturday. The many public holidays also close the shops. So beware!

Here are a few phrases to start you off on your shopping in France:

Good morning	**Bonjour**
Good evening	**Bonsoir**
Please	**S'il vous plaît**
Thank you	**Merci**
Please can I have ... kilos of ...?	**Donnez-moi ... kilos de ..., s'il vous plaît**
That's too expensive	**C'est trop cher**
Give me a little more, please	**Donnez-en moi encore, s'il vous plaît**
Give me a little less, please	**Donnez-en moi moins, s'il vous plaît**
Please will you cut it for me?	**Coupez-le, s'il vous plaît**
Please will you clean it for me?	**Nettoyez-le, s'il vous plaît**

1	**un**
2	**deux**
3	**trois**
4	**quatre**
5	**cinq**
6	**six**
7	**sept**
8	**huit**
9	**neuf**
10	**dix**
100	**cent**
1000	**mille**
500 g ($\frac{1}{2}$ kg)	**une livre**
half	**demi**
quarter	**quart**

The Fishmonger   **La Poissonnerie**

To cater for the French love of fish there is a good fishmonger in every seaside town and village and, inland, in any town of reasonable size. In France, you will come across familiar North Atlantic fish, as well as those from warmer Atlantic waters and the Mediterranean.

Le poissonnier the fishmonger sells all types of sea and freshwater fish, shellfish and molluscs. It is usually attractively displayed, fresh and clean with each item clearly marked with its name and price per unit – usually per kilo; for the whole fish *la pièce*, a fillet *filet*, a steak *une tranche*; or per 100 grams for the smallest shellfish like shrimps; per dozen *douze* for the more expensive molluscs like oysters; by the litre measure *en mesure* or *par litre* for the smaller molluscs like mussels and cockles; and finally by 'everything on a plate' which is *le plateau complet* or just *le tout*. Freshwater fish, like trout and carp, are sometimes sold live *vivant* from a tank.

Also sold, sometimes given away, are the herbs to go with the fish like fennel, parsley and lemons but only if you buy your fish there.

anchovy	**anchois** similar to a sardine but with a large mouth
angler fish	**lotte de mer** or **baudroie** very ugly fish, all mouth and teeth with three 'filaments' on its outsized head. Grey–brown in colour, the tail is good eating
bass, sea	**bar, loup de mer** silvery fish with grey–blue backs and white bellies
bream, gilthead	**daurade, dorade** bluish-white back, silver–yellow flanks and white belly. Sometimes called golden eyebrow because of a brilliant yellow crescent between the eyes
brill	**barbue** flatfish with a dull grey–yellow back
carp	**carpe** a freshwater toothless fish with a dark brown back
clams	**palourdes** large smooth mollusc **praires** rough-shelled. Sold by the dozen *douze*
cockles	**coques** known as the poor man's oyster or **bucarde sourdon** on the Atlantic coast
cod	**cabillaud**
crayfish	**langonste** like a lobster with no claws
crayfish, freshwater	**écrevisse** with pincers, small, grey–blue, expensive

dentex	**denté** silver with steel-blue back and reddish tint to fins. Expensive
Dublin Bay prawns	**langoustines** like tiny lobsters but with long arms and pincers rather than claws
eel	**anguille** usually sold alive, dark brown in colour. It is best to ask the fishmonger to prepare them for you as skimming is difficult
eel, conger	**anguille de mer** very dangerous fish when alive but good eating, the conger has pale grey skin and white flesh and is sold in steaks
flounder	**flet** an oval flatfish, light brown with pale orange spots. Should have a little slime on the back when fresh
gurnard	**grondin, rouget-grondin** may be erroneously bought as red mullet as it is also pale pink in colour. It has a large 'armour-plated' head and a small tapering body
haddock	**aiglefin** similar in appearance to a cod but has a distinctive dark 'smudge' behind the gills
hake	**colin** long round slender fish with silver–grey scales. Sold whole, in cutlets or fillets. Sometimes served up as *saumon blanc* on menus
halibut	**flétan** large flatfish from northern France, dark olive in colour with a marbled skin and firm white flesh
herring	**hareng** silver–grey–blue fish with oily flesh
	hareng fumé smoked herring, a great speciality of Boulogne
John Dory	**dorée, saint Pierre, poule de mer** an oval fish with a spiny head easily recognizable from the black spot on either side circled in grey on the gills
lamprey	**lamproie** eel-shaped, dirty green–brown with black blotches all over the body. Sold in steaks

lobster	**homard** dark blue when alive, red when cooked. Make sure the lobster is alive up to the point of cooking
mackerel	**maquereau** dark blue back with bright blue–green stripes and a silver belly. Cheap and plentiful
mullet, grey	**mulet** grey scaly fish with distinct lines down the side and a silvery white belly
mullet, red	**rouget, rouget-barbet** this pink-to-red fish is common and plentiful and very good eating. Most rose-coloured fish are called *rouget* but only the true red mullet have two barbules hanging from their lower jaws (unlike gurnard)
mussels	**moules** cultivated mussels **de bouchot** are better than the wild varieties and can be distinguished by convex outside edge. **Moules d'Espagne** the best
oysters	**huîtres** wild or more commonly cultivated. The green **Marennes** oysters are fattened with a special algae; Portuguese oysters are cheaper, have a rough shell and are larger than the others
perch	**perche** the best freshwater fish with a bright green back, golden yellow flanks. Artificially bred and sometimes sold alive
pike	**brochet** very popular freshwater fish, dark green with ugly protruding jaw and rows of sharp teeth
	quenelles de brochet pike dumplings are sold already made up
plaice	**carrelet, plie franche** brown flatfish with bright orange spots that fade with age
prawns	**crevettes roses**
sardines	**sardines** silver fish with a grey–blue back, common and cheap in the Mediterranean and Atlantic. Also known as **cardeau** and **poutine** in south France, where they are much liked

scallops	**coquilles Saint Jacques** large pinkish brown shells with a bright orange roe. Common, sold alive
scorpion fish	**rascasse** oblong, ugly fish with a high back and spiny head, poisonous spikes and black marks on a grey skin. The basis of the fish soup *bouillabaisse*
shrimps	**crevettes** common and plentiful
skate	**raie** only the 'wings' are sold, in steaks
sole, Dover	**sole** oval flatfish with hard, tiny scales. Olive-brown with black markings. It is essential to remove the inedible skin
sole, lemon	**sole-limande** similar in appearance to a sole but with a smooth skin and is inferior in taste although much cheaper (do not confuse with inferior dab **limande**)
squid	**calmar** soft white elongated bodies
trout	**truite** brown speckled fish now all artificially bred and usually sold alive
tunny	**thon** blue-backed silvery spindle-shaped fish, usually large and sold in steaks
turbot	**turbot** large grey–brown flatfish with spines on the back and dotted with black, sometimes white, marks
whitebait	**blanchaille** the fry of the herring or sprat mostly caught in the Channel, silver and about 4 cm/1½ in. long
whiting	**merlan** grey–green fish, adequate white flesh, and inexpensive

The Butcher   **La Boucherie**

In France each animal and bird seems to have its own particular seller. Lamb, mutton, beef and veal are sold in the *boucherie*. Pork, both raw and cooked, is sold in the *charcuterie*, together with sausages, salamis and those delicious savouries and salads. Chicken comes from a *marchand de volailles*, game and goat from a *marchand de gibier*. Finally there is the *boucherie chevaline*, the horsemeat shop, where few tourists will be tempted, although the meat is said to be comparable with beef and much less expensive. This shop is easily recognized by a red horse's head over the door. Many smaller towns do not have such a wide range of shops but most have a *boucherie*, selling all meat except horse, a *charcuterie* that also sells poultry and game and a *boucherie chevaline*. (By law horsemeat can only be sold in a licensed *boucherie chevaline* so there is no chance of buying it by mistake.)

Beef **Boeuf**

Beef in France is good but expensive. The method of butchering is slightly different to the English but there are usually near equivalents to our own cuts. Their joints are well trimmed and all roasting joints will be larded with bacon or pork fat and tied ready for cooking.

brisket	**poitrine**
châteaubriand	**châteaubriand** the best and most expensive cut
chuck end	**paleron**
covered ribs	**côte couverte** usually rolled and good value
fillet steak	**filet**
flank	**hampe**
leg	**crosse**
neck	**jumeaux**
ribs	**plat de côte**
rump steak	**aiguillette**
shin	**gîte de devant** or **gîte de derrière**
silverside	**gîte à la noix**
sirloin	**contre filet** or **faux filet** either tied ready for roasting or cut in steaks – **entrecôte**
top side	**tende de tranche**

Veal　**Veau**

Veal can be the very expensive milk-fed calf but is now more likely to be baby beef.

belly	**ventre**
best end of neck	**carré**
breast	**poitrine**
chump end of loin	**cul** or **quasi**
fillet end of leg	**rouelle**
knuckle	**jarret**
loin	**longe**
shoulder	**épaule**
topside	**noix**

Goat　**Chèvre**

In France goats are raised primarily for milk. Only kids are eaten, usually at Easter or some other special occasion. The meat is good but expensive, and tends to be tougher than lamb. If not sold whole the cuts are similar to lamb cuts.

Lamb　**Agneau**

Lamb is as expensive as beef but mutton *mouton* is a little cheaper.

baron	**baron d'agneau** almost the whole of the rear end of the lamb with both legs, tail and back
best end of neck	**côte première** or **côte seconde** chops from either back of lamb or the neck end
leg	**gigot d'agneau**
loin chop	**côte de filet** really somewhere between a loin chop and a chump chop
rack	**carré d'agneau**
saddle	**selle d'agneau** cut from the back end of the lamb either as double chops or tied as a roast
shoulder	**épaule** a good buy as a cheaper cut and usually boned and rolled for roasting, either *épaule roulée* or *en ballon*

Poultry and Game   **Volailles et Gibier**
Game and chickens can sometimes be bought in the *boucherie* but a
marchand de gibier, for game, and a *marchand de volailles*, for poultry, is
a common stall in most markets. Chicken is comparatively cheap
and excellent quality as it is usually 'free range'. It often comes
whole, so ask the butcher to clean the bird and cut its head off for
.you! (*Coupez la tête s'il vous plâit.*)

chicken	**poulet** the collective name for all chickens. Choose those with small uniform combs and elastic flesh
	poussin very small birds, enough for one person
	poularde a large old boiler
	poulet de grain maize-fed with distinct yellow flesh
	poulet gras fat chicken
duck	**canard** all artificially bred. Avoid those under 1.5 kg/3¾ lb
frogs' legs	**cuisses de grenouille** mostly imported from Central Europe, expensive and not very common now
guinea fowl	**pintade** now solely bred for the table, it has a distinct grey plumage spotted with white; guinea chick *pintadeau* is excellent and is found in the markets in July
hare	**lièvre** quite common in the markets. Buy a young hare *capucin* – male up to 1 year or female up to 2 years. Young hares have slender paws and smooth coats and their ears tear easily while older hares have wavy coats and splayed feet. Ask the butcher to skin the hare, and take a jar with a good lid for the blood. Not expensive and good value, but too rich to eat in hot weather
partridge	**perdreau** are the younger birds
	perdrix are the older birds. Either grey partridge or the red-legged partridge; both good but expensive

rabbit	**lapin** common and inexpensive. Choose young rabbits which can be recognized by their short necks, plump knees and front legs that move in all directions
quail	**caille** common and inexpensive as bred in huge quantities; always sold dressed
snails	**escargots** the vineyard snails are considered the best; now usually sold already prepared with garlic butter
turkey	**dindon** hen birds *dindes* are better
venison	**venaison** not uncommon in wild districts or else in cities

Le marchand d'abats sells offal *abats* only but it is more often found in a *boucherie*.

brains	**cervelles**
calf's foot	**pied de veau**
kidneys	**rognons**
liver	**foie**
sweetbreads (calves')	**ris de veau**
tongue (fresh)	**langue**
tripe	**tripes**

The Pork Butcher and the Delicatessen
La Charcuterie

There is a saying that every morsel of a pig, from snout to tail, can be eaten, a saying borne out by the endless pork cuts and sausages, both fresh and preserved, to be found in the *charcuterie*, surely the national shop of France. The French housewife relies on it, buying there not only her pork *porc* and allied products, but also other cooked meats (pâtés, terrines, cooked chickens, etc.), delicious vol-au-vents and prepared salads, the best of the *épicerie* – eggs, cheeses, and other products – and sometimes fresh chicken and game as well. Very often there is a red pig's head over the door.

All meat in France is expensive but pork is good value and considerably less expensive than beef.

Pork	**Porc**
bacon, streaky	**petit lard**, **lard maigre**
belly	**poitrine** a cheap cut, but nonetheless good for roasting when boned

hand	**plat de côtes** a cheaper cut for roasting
leg	**jambon** the more expensive upper half of the leg that is good for roasting
	jambonneau lower part of leg or knuckle
loin	**carré** similar to the best end of pork or cutlets. A single chop is *côte de porc*
loin	**filet** both the fillet and tenderloin, excellent but expensive
neck end	**échine** this cut also includes the shoulder and the spare rib chops – not ribs at all
	palette a roasting joint from the top of the shoulder
salt pork	**porc salé**
trotters	**pieds**

Other cooked meats

black pudding	**boudin noir** a blood sausage
chitterlings	**andouilles** hard, spiced, smoked sausage, made from pork and pork offal
dried sausages	**saucissons secs** pork sausages that differ from one region to another
	rosettes spicy hard sausage with a thick pork fat skin that flavours the meat
garlic sausages	**saucissons d'ail**
ham	**jambon** there are many different ways of curing ham in France, including:
	jambon de Bayonne salted, cured and dried on the bone. Should be cut wafer thin, excellent but expensive
	jambon de York York ham, cooked and without bone
	noix de jambon a round, boned smoked ham
meat loaf	**terrine** coarsely cut baked meat, mixed and spiced in the style of a region
	terrine de gibier game terrine
pâté	**pâté** made in various shapes and sizes; usually in long or round shapes like a loaf or in earthenware pots, and sold by the 100 grams. Common types include:

	pâté de campagne coarse-cut meat and spices mixed to a distinctive regional recipe
	pâté de canard duck pâté
	pâté de dinde turkey pâté
	pâté de foie pure liver pâté with a smooth creamy texture
	pâté de jambon ham pâté
	pâté de lapin rabbit pâté
	pâté de lièvre hare pâté
	pâté de tête, **fromage de tête** pig's-head pâté or brawn
pottage	**rillettes** usually soft, ground mixture of pork and pork fat, mainly from Normandy
	rillettes de lapin made from rabbit
	rillettes d'oie made from goose
salami	**salami** both French and Italian salamis are common
sausages	**saucisses** there are as many different sausages as there are regions or even districts, in France

There are literally hundreds of different salads *salades* sold throughout France. Here are four of the more common:

artichauts à la Grecque artichokes in vinaigrette dressing
champignons à la Grecque button mushrooms with a vinaigrette and onion dressing
salade de pommes de terre potato salad in mayonnaise
salade niçoise hard boiled eggs, anchovy fillets, black olives, capers and vinaigrette dressing

The Cheeseshop   **La Fromagerie**

'How can one govern a country,' asked General de Gaulle, 'that produces 246 different cheeses?' With such a wide range of soil and climate in France and so many breeds of cattle, sheep and goats it is hardly surprising that there are so many varieties. The French are passionately fond of, and knowledgeable about, their cheeses – consequently there is always a large selection of mature cheeses to be bought. Only the big towns have separate cheese shops

Cheeses

fromageries; elsewhere cheeses are found on market stalls, in the *charcuterie* or the *supermarché*. They can be divided into six basic types

FRESH CREAM CHEESE
Mostly from Normandy where they originated, these cheeses are made entirely from cows' milk.

petit Suisse instantly recognizable in its small cylindrical corrugated pot, this creamy, unsalted cheese is delicious on its own, with sugar or with fruit

demi sel similar to petit Suisse but less creamy, salted and square in shape

boursin and other herb cheeses are produced all over France. A basic cream cheese with garlic, chives and pepper and a selection of other herbs

SOFT CHEESES

The three types of soft cheese are distinguishable by the rind – floury, washed and natural. All of them are strong, the riper the cheese the stronger.

Floury rind either chalky white or, when matured, brown
Brie acknowledged for centuries as the king of all cheeses. Smooth texture with edible white rind and of incomparable taste. The best variety is Brie de Meaux. They are bought whole, up to 45 cm/18 in. in diameter or in slices by the 100 grams. Test for ripeness by pressing the top of the cheese, which should be springy
Camembert small round cheese, no more than 10 cm/4 in. in diameter. Strong flavour when ripe, it is sold all over France

Washed rind this process gives the cheese a smooth and glossy skin, either straw yellow or brick red
Pont l'Évêque a square cheese, golden inside with rich bronze rind. When fresh the cheese sticks to the knife
Livarot, Munster and **Reblochon** are others

Naturally formed crust mostly goats' milk cheese
Banon small cheese made from goats' milk, cured and sold in chestnut leaves
Picodon farm cheese made from goats' milk with keen flavour and pale yellow skin. Sold in grey clay pots
Saint Maure, **Olivet** and **Crottin** are others

SEMI-HARD CHEESES

These contain little water so store well. They should always be kept covered with a damp cloth.

Cantal hard, strong cows' milk cheese from the Auvergne similar to a true Cheddar in texture and shape
Saint Paulin or **Port Salut** round cheese 20 cm/8 in. in diameter with smooth orange rind and creamy yellow soft inside. Made and sold all over France
Saint-Nectaire and **Tome de Savoie** are two others

HARD CHEESES

Generally very large cheeses, quite often with holes. They have a natural hard crust and hard inside, and are sold in segments by the

100 grams. Always keep the pieces covered to prevent a second rind forming.

Emmental a hard yellow cheese shaped like a mill stone with pronounced holes
Beaufort slightly bland in taste, this cheese has a dull gold inside and is lightly salted. Similar to Swiss Gruyère
Comté so similar to Gruyère that it is called *Gruyère de Comté* and is easily recognized by the mass of bubbles

VEINED OR BLUE CHEESES
Made from either cows' or ewes' milk with a mould culture (*penecillium roqueforti*) introduced during the maturing period.

Roquefort the best-known blue cheese has a pungent tang to its crumbly, salty texture. It is made from ewes' milk and sold all over France
Bleu de Bresse, Bleu des Causses and **Bleu d'Auvergne** are others

PROCESSED CHEESES
These cheeses are mild and creamy, pre-packed in foil or covered in grape-pips, walnuts or almonds

The Dairy   **La Crèmerie**

The dairy on its own is really a shop of the past – to be found, like the cheese shops, only in the larger towns and cities. Usually it has merged with the market cheese-stall or the *charcuterie*, or been taken over by the *supermarché*.

butter	**beurre** all butter sold in France is unsalted except in the north-west (Normandy and Brittany) where **beurre salé** salted butter is produced and sometimes sent to other parts of France
cream	**crème fraîche** not at all like the single or double cream found in Britain but slightly soured

eggs	**oeufs** sold by the dozen or half-dozen, they are mostly from battery hens but fine free-range eggs are not uncommon in the country markets
milk	**lait** usually sold in cartons of one or a half-litre
yoghurt	**yaourt**

The Grocer   L'Épicerie

Unlike many of the specialized shops in France the *épicerie* has remained the same, unaffected by the challenge of the supermarket *supermarché*. It continues to sell a wide selection of dry goods including the more unusual and exotic tinned foods, jams, wines and spirits. Also found in the *épicerie* are pastries, bread and dairy products as well as pâtés and some delicatessen items.

breadcrumbs	**chapelures**
capers	**câpres**
cayenne pepper	**poivre de cayenne**
chocolate	**chocolat** cooking chocolate is very bitter and sold in slabs
cloves	**cloux de girofles**
coffee	**café** dozens of blends and brands to suit all tastes are sold already ground or in beans
cornflower	**fécule de maïs**
curry powder	**cari, kari**
figs, dried	**figues sèches** often flavoured with caraway seeds
flour	**farine**
gelatine	**gélatine**
honey	**miel**
jam	**confiture**

lentils	**lentilles** small red or grey dried bean seeds
macaroni	**macaroni**
mineral water	**eau minérale**
mushrooms, dried	**champignons secs** widely used in French cookery. The black are very strong, the cream or light brown ones less so
mustard	**moutarde** one of the oldest ingredients in French cooking. It is made from mustard flour, grape must (unfermented grape juice) or vinegar with a selection of herbs and spices. The best-known are the mustards of Dijon, which come in sturdy 1-kilo glass jars and cost astonishingly little. Buy one to take home!
noodles	**nouilles**
nutmeg	**noix de Muscade**
oil, olive	**huile d'olive**
oil, sunflower	**huile de girasol**
oil, vegetable	**huile de cuisine**
olives	**olives** either green **vertes**, pickled unripe in brine, or black **noires**, pickled ripe in best olive oil
pasta	**pasta** all names are the same as for Italy (pages 142–3)
pastry, frozen	**pâte congelé**
pepper	**poivre** now sold only packaged, either black or white
peppercorns	**poivre en grains**
prunes	**pruneaux**
raisins	**raisin secs**
	raisins de Malaga extra large, delicious and eaten as a dessert
rice	**riz**
rice, patna (long grain)	**riz caroline**
salt	**sel; sel gemme** rock salt; **sel gris** or **gros sel** coarse, partially-refined salt; **sel marin** sea salt
salt cod	**morue**
sugar	**sucre; sucre glace** icing sugar; **sucre en poudre** caster sugar

tea	**thé** is drunk in France, although only a small selection of types is usually available, most of them English
tomato purée	**purée de tomates**
toothpicks	**cure-dents**
vanilla	**vanille** sold in essence, although sometimes the black pods are available
vinegar	**vinaigre: vinaigre de vin** wine vinegar; **vinaigre de cidre** cider vinegar; **vinaigre d'estragon** tarragon vinegar
yeast	**levure** usually the powdered variety but in some of the more remote areas live yeast is sold from the bakery

The Baker   **La Boulangerie**
The Pastry Shop   **La Pâtisserie**
The Cakeshop   **La Confiserie**

The French take their bread very seriously. Every town and village has its quota of excellent bakers, sometimes selling only bread but

Bread & Patisserie

more usually now combining all three trades. They sell all shapes, sizes and colours of bread, lovely pastries neatly set out on trays, fruit flans and wonderful sticky cakes. Even in the small towns they usually bake twice a day, so you should buy fresh bread for lunch and again for supper. French bread is marvellous fresh, and goes stale in less than a day. Rotas are arranged so that you can almost always find a breadshop open on Sundays and Mondays, at least up to mid-day.

By law a list of bread *pain* sold, with prices, must be displayed in the windows of all bakeries. Prices are both per kilo and *la pièce*. The baker will cut a loaf, but more often than not there is a size to suit your needs.

baguette (**Parisienne**) long thin crispy loaf with diagonal scoring on top
bâtard identical in content to *baguette* but shorter and fatter
brioche a cake made from yeast dough, usually shaped in a ball with a smaller ball pressed on top. Usually the size of a bread roll (but can be larger to be stuffed). Wonderful hot for breakfast with plenty of butter
croissant literally 'crescent' – a roll made with puff pastry in that shape. Another breakfast treat hot with butter
ficelle half a *bâtard* but shorter and fatter
ficelle Viennoise a Vienna loaf rather like a milk loaf
pain complet or **pain au son** considered an inferior loaf as the flour contains bran. Good and wholesome, it is round or oval
pain de campagne country bread made from wholemeal wheat. Expensive but good, usually oval and scored on top
pain de seigle rye bread dark brown in colour
pain Italien another wheat loaf oval in shape
petit pain a smaller Vienna loaf like a long roll
petit pain au chocolat a small roll with chocolate inside

The pastry shop *pâtisserie* is one of the great delights of France, with the variety and unrivalled excellence of its products. Everything is sold by the piece or, for smaller items, 100 grams. You can also buy empty pastry cases *moules* for your own tarts or *quiches*.

amandine almond biscuits
éclairs long thin choux pastry cases filled with either fresh cream, **crème fraîche** or a rich, thickened custard **crème pâtissière** topped with either milk or bitter chocolate
florentine biscuit with chocolate on one side, nuts on the other

gâteau the word covers all types of cake
gâteau praliné buttered cream sponge cake with almonds
jalousie a flaky pastry with almond flavour
mille-feuilles 'thousand leaves': flaky pastry filled with cream and jam with icing sugar on top
moka sponge cake with coffee buttered cream
mont blanc chestnut purée with fresh cream
Paris-Brest pastry filled with chocolate cream
petits fours small round almond paste biscuits with either almond, cherry or walnut on top. Sold by the 100 grams
religieuse supposedly it resembles a nun, one ball on top of the other with a chocolate 'habit', cream face and wimple!
Saint Honoré choux pastry filled with chocolate and cream
tarte aux pommes apple tart; **aux abricots** apricot tart; **aux prunes** plum tart
truffe au rhum rum truffles: rich chocolate balls covered with cocoa

The Greengrocer   **Le Marchand de Légumes**

Agriculture, with market gardening and fruit farming, is the largest single industry in France, which means that there is always a constant supply of fresh and varied fruits and vegetables.

artichokes	**artichauts** globes with stiff, green overlapping leaves. The purple baby artichokes can be eaten raw
asparagus	**asperges** expensive, sold in bundles by the kilo in the spring. **Argenteuil** the best variety
aubergine or egg plant	**aubergine** sometimes they are small, oval and white like an egg but usually large, deep purple and pendulous
avocado pear	**avocat** green, sometimes purple, knobbly and pear-shaped with green waxy flesh
basil	**basilic** a common herb sold fresh by the bunch
bay leaves	**feuilles de laurier** sold by the bunch
beans, broad	**fèves**
beans, field	**féveroles** slightly smaller than broad beans

beans, french	**haricots verts** light green or pale yellow, quite fat with prominent seeds
beans, green	**flageolets** small greenish beans, either dried or fresh, commonly served with meat dishes
beans, white	**haricots blancs** similar to french beans but white
beetroot	**betterave**
Brussels sprouts	**choux de Bruxelles**
cabbage	**chou** either smooth-leaved, Milan cabbage (with curly leaves) or red cabbage
carrots	**carottes**
cauliflower	**choufleur** sometimes sold with its edible leaves
celeriac	**céleri-rave** the root, between an apple and coconut in size, has a brown fibrous skin and creamy white flesh that tastes of celery. A winter vegetable – also in autumn if you are lucky
celery	**céleri**
chard	**bettes**, **blettes** related to the beetroot but used for its leaves like spinach (**cardes** or **côtes de blettes** refers to the white rib or stem)
chervil	**cerfeuil** one of the more common herbs and the basis of *fines herbes*. Sold fresh by the bunch
chicory	**endive** a French teaser as the names are reversed in English and French! A salad vegetable with a conical head and tight greenish-white leaves
chives	**ciboulettes**, **civettes**, **cives** much used in salads and sold by the bunch
courgettes	**courgettes** vegetable-marrow harvested when only 15 cm/6 in. long
cucumber	**concombre**
dandelion leaves	**pissenlits** the French eat the young tender leaves of this common weed
endive	**chicorée** a salad vegetable similar to lettuce but with pale green, almost yellow leaves that are frizzled and bitter

escarole	**scarole** similar to endive with wide dark green leaves although sometimes white when grown in the dark
fennel	**fenouil** an aromatic flowering plant with a bulbous stem. The feathery tops are used for seasoning. Pale green and white in colour, the darker green ones should be avoided
garlic	**ail** an essential part of French cooking it is sold by the head *la tête* (a clove is *gousse*)
leeks	**poireaux**
lettuce	**laitue** comes in a great variety of shapes and sizes
marjoram	**marjolaine** an aromatic herb sold by the bunch
mushrooms	**champignons** cultivated mushrooms **champignons de couches** are either button, cup or flat according to age. The many varieties of wild mushrooms are considered great delicacies in France, but there are equally as many that are deadly poisonous. Any chemist should tell you whether mushrooms are edible or not
onions	**oignons**
parsley	**persil**, **persil frisé** the common curly-leaved variety of parsley **persil à la grosse racine** variety with an edible stalk
peas	**pois** peas; **petits pois** little peas; **mange-tout** peas in flat pods eaten whole
peppers, sweet	**piments doux**
potatoes	**pommes de terre**
pumpkin	**potiron** a gourd with bright orange flesh and a distinctive sweet flavour. Sold whole or by the piece
radishes	**radis** sold in bunches
rosemary	**romarin** leaf herb found mostly in Provence
sage	**sauge** sold by the bunch

salsify	**salsifis** long, pointed, brown roots with soft white flesh when peeled. Choose those with grey–green leaves and even tapering roots
shallots	**échalottes** like small onions and with a slight garlic flavour
spinach	**épinard**
tarragon	**estragon** typical French herb, widely used and sold by the bunch
thyme	**thym** another common herb sold by the bunch
tomatoes	**tomates**
turnips	**navets** common vegetable sold all year round
vine leaves	**feuilles de vigne** used to wrap up fish for cooking or when young finely chopped in salads
watercress	**cresson** sold by the bunch. Eat straight away

The Fruit Shop   Le Marchand de Fruits

Practically all fruit is sold by the kilo.

almonds	**amandes** either bitter or sweet, spring almonds are sold green and eaten whole
apples	**pommes**
apricots	**abricots** an Armenian fruit brought to France in fifteenth century
bananas	**bananes** imported from the French West Indies
cherries	**cerises**
chestnuts	**marrons** collecting chestnuts in the autumn is almost a national sport
coconut	**noix de coco**
dates	**dattes**
figs	**figues**
grapefruit	**pamplemousse** sold individually, *la pièce*
grapes	**raisins** sold by the kilo, dessert grapes are either black or green; *Muscatel* grapes are golden and scented

greengages	**reines claudes** with a red tinge to the greenish-yellow skin, a plentiful second summer fruit
hazel nuts	**noisettes**
lemons	**citrons** abundant and cheap
melon, cantaloup	**melon cantaloup** greenish-yellow skin, rather squashed in shape with succulent yellow–orange flesh
melon, charentais	**melon charentais** small and perfectly round, yellow–green rough skin with even indentations and succulent scented orange flesh
melon, honeydew	**melon d'Espagne** oval in shape, wrinkled green, yellow or white skin and light green flesh
melon, water	**melon d'eau** very large and thus sold by the piece it has a dark green skin, red watery flesh and a mass of jet black pips
oranges	**oranges** all good eating but navel oranges, with a hole at the top, are the best
peaches	**pêches** first summer fruit, either yellow or white flesh. The white is better eating and the yellow are later in the season
pears	**poires** in season from summer to Christmas
pineapple	**ananas** imported from the French West Indies and sold by *la pièce*
plums	**prunes** either red or dark blue–black, they are cheap and plentiful all summer
raspberries	**framboises** excellent but expensive even in season
walnuts	**noix** sold in packets when imported, loose by the kilo when locally grown

Wines and Spirits

Wines

French wines are the best in the world. This is no accident: France is the perfect wine-growing country with all the right ingredients:

ideal soil, expert wine-growers *vignerons*, strict government and growers' quality controls, a tremendous range of climate – and a national passion about wine.

The simplest way to condense all the heavy tomes on wines to a 'thumbnail sketch' is to explain the information given on the label.

Colour is either *rouge* (red), *blanc* (white) or *rosé* (rose or pink).

Taste is either *sec* (dry), *doux* (sweet) or *demi-sec* (medium dry).

The **date** shows when the wine was produced, the year of the vintage. Cheaper blended wines are not dated.

The **name of the wine** or the **region** where it was produced. There are nine regions:

Bordeaux, probably the best-known region, produces both red, full-bodied and smooth wines like *Médoc* and *Pomerol* (all known in England as claret), and white wines like *Entre-deux-Mers* and the sweet *Sauternes*.

Burgundy produces both the smooth powerful red wines such as *Bourgogne*, *Beaune* and *Nuits Saint-Georges* and the delicate white wines like *Chablis* and *Pouilly Fuissé*.

Beaujolais is a fine red wine drunk young – *Beaujolais*, *Fleurie*.

Côtes du Rhône is either a robust red wine matured through long summers like *Châteauneuf du Pape*, or rosé like *Tavel*.

The Loire valley produces light, dry, summer white wines like *Vouvray* or less dry wines like *Muscadet*, also the well-known rosé *Anjou* and the red *Touraine*.

Alsace is well-known for fruity white wines like *Riesling* and *Sylvaner*.

Provence's wine like her cooking is robust – such as the red *Côtes de Provence*. Also white and rosé.

Languedoc and *Roussillon* produce more quantity than quality. The home of the everyday drinking wines like the *vins de pays*.

Champagne should need no introduction! It will have the name of the champagne house on the bottle, for example *Charles Heidsieck*.

Mis en bouteille dans la région means that it has been bottled where it was produced.

Appellation controlée (*A C*) and **V D Q S** (*Vin Délimité de Qualité Supérieure*) guarantee that the wine conforms with the strict controls of origin and quality.

Vin de pays and **Vin de table** are the everyday drinking wines. *Vin de pays* is superior to *vin de table* which is usually blended, often with Italian wine, and sold under a trade name. When wine is bought by the litre, bottles marked with stars round neck are returnable: small deposit paid.

Château or **Domaine** is the particular vineyard where the wine is produced – these wines are usually rather special.

Apéritifs

An *apéritif* is a common drink before a meal in France. It can simply be a glass of wine; try white wine and soda or Perrier water served in a long glass with ice. Another good mixture if you like blackcurrants is *Kir* – white wine and a little *Crème de Cassis*, served very cold. If you like aniseed you are well catered for in France with brands like *Pernod* and *Ricard* that are mixed with water.

Spirits

There is a wealth of spirits and liqueurs (*digestifs*) for after dinner: the fine brandies *Cognac* and *Armagnac*; the liqueurs of the monks, *Bénédictine* and *Chartreuse*, and the well-known *Crème de Menthe* – 'sticky green' tasting of peppermint. Among liqueurs sadly less common in England are *Calvados*, made from the excellent cider produced in Normandy, and *Marc* – a rather fiery spirit made from the residue of the wine pressings in Savoie.

COOKING

It is a common fallacy that French cooking is rich, elaborate, complex – and difficult. *Haute cuisine*, the sophisticated cooking of intricate dishes with expensive ingredients, can be all of these things – but not the everyday cooking of *cuisine bourgeoise*, and the simpler peasant cooking of the provinces that relies on the local produce and wine.

What is true is that the French have a traditional care and reverence for food, expecting to pay perhaps a little more when buying it, to take a little more care and time in preparing it, and (not least) to spend a little more time enjoying the eating of it. French produce is usually excellent – not least because the shopkeeper expects you will want the very best.

For the self-catering visitor it is the regional cookery, the simpler dishes of local ingredients, that matter. Brittany (*Bretagne* – do not confuse with *Grande Bretagne*!) and Normandy, in the north-west of France, are rich in sea food, milk and butter, as well as apples and cider. Further south in the Bordeaux country alongside the famous wine are some of the best beef cattle, *Limousin*. South again, in the

Basque country, is the home of the spiced sausages, and the Mediterranean south, Provence, gives its name to all dishes with an oil, garlic and tomato base. The east has a strong German flavour, while central France boasts fine wines and some of the best cooking in France around Lyon.

Crème vichyssoise   Cold leek soup

Simple – and classic – cold soup. Serves 6.

100 g/4 oz butter	*5 medium potatoes, peeled and*
4 leeks – the white part only,	*cubed very small*
chopped very small	*1 small carton (150 ml)* crème
1 onion, finely chopped	fraiche *(cream)*
1¹/₂ litres/2¹/₂ pints chicken or other	*chives or parsley, chopped*
white stock	*pinch of nutmeg*

Heat the butter in a heavy saucepan and add the leeks and onions. Cook until a soft golden colour. Add the chicken stock and potatoes. Bring to the boil and simmer gently, uncovered, for 40 minutes, stirring occasionally.

Pass through a sieve (if you have one), or crush the pieces of potato between the back of a spoon and the side of the saucepan. Allow to cool.

Stir in the cream, chives or parsley and nutmeg. Season with pepper and salt.

Serve chilled from the refrigerator.

Céleri-rave remoulade   Celeriac and mayonnaise

The lumpy round brown root of celeriac does not look attractive, but it is an excellent vegetable and justly esteemed in France. It has a taste like celery. Mostly a winter vegetable, you will find it in spring and autumn if you are lucky. 1 large or 2 small celeriacs are ample for 4 people.

celeriac
mayonnaise (page 203)

Peel the celeriac, and cut in thin slices. Cut across these slices finely again so you have a great many thin strips about the size and thickness of a match. Cook them in boiling salted water for just 2 minutes and drain: they are done when they are beginning to soften but still a little crunchy. Allow to cool.

Mix the celeriac with enough mayonnaise to coat each stick.

Serve as a starter by itself, or with thin slices of smoked ham or salami.

Another excellent celeriac dish is York ham *jambon de York*, painted with Dijon mustard *moutarde de Dijon* rolled round a celeriac filling. Celeriac can also be eaten raw, if it is grated and then mixed with mayonnaise.

Salsifis   Salsify

Salsify is an excellent vegetable and terribly easy to prepare. ½ kg/1 lb is plenty for 4. It is served cold with mayonnaise (page 203) as a starter, or hot as a vegetable.

salsify
butter

Wash the salsify and cut it in half if large. Keep the leaves. Boil it in salted water for 30 minutes and remove. When it is cool enough to handle peel off the thick brown skin, and cut the salsify into sections about 8 cm/3 in. long. Melt the butter in the pan and heat the salsify, shaking from time to time so it is heated through.

Serve immediately with the chopped leaves to garnish, or leave to serve cold.

Escargots   Snails

For those determined to adopt the true flavour of France I am including these directions for cooking snails. Buy snails that have been prepared with garlic butter, and allow between 9 and a dozen per person. Beg, buy or borrow the special snail dishes *escargotières*, or use a metal oven dish.

Place the snails, open end upwards, in the dish (one to each indentation if it is an *escargotière*), and bake in a moderate oven for about 20 minutes or until bubbling. Serve them straight away. Eat with special snail pincers and forks (if you have them) or with ordinary forks, dunking the snails and fresh bread in the garlic butter.

Salade niçoise

This salad is very filling and makes an ideal light lunch. Although the recipe looks long, it is easy to prepare. You can dispense with some of the ingredients if they are not available – indeed, any combination of the main ingredients makes a good salad in its own right. The quantities make plenty for 6 as a starter, or for 4 as a main course.

2 eggs
225 g/¹/₂ lb french beans
¹/₄ cucumber
1 green pepper
6 tablespoons vinaigrette dressing
(page 203)
the heart of a lettuce

the heart of an endive
1 chicory
1 small can (around 200 g/8 oz)
tunny (tuna fish – thon)
1 small tin anchovy fillets
2 tomatoes
10 black olives, stoned

Hard-boil the eggs (8 to 10 minutes). Peel and cut into quarters. Top and tail the french beans (string the sides if they are past their first youth), and slice into pieces not more than 7 cm/2½ in. long. Boil them in a little salted water for around 7 minutes, drain and allow to cool. Score the sides of the cucumber with a fork and slice very thinly. Seed the green pepper and slice thinly.

Pour the vinaigrette into a large salad bowl. Add the french beans. Break into small pieces with your hands the lettuce, endive and chicory, and place gently in the bowl. Break the tunny into largish pieces and add to the bowl. Drain the oil off the anchovies and add them to the bowl. Finally, add the tomatoes, eggs, pepper, cucumber and olives.

As soon as possible after making the salad toss the mixture (use your hands) so all the ingredients are well covered with the dressing and thoroughly mixed. Serve at once, as the dressing will make the lettuce limp if it is left.

Quiche lorraine Egg and bacon flan

One of the great simple dishes of France. It can be easily adapted by substituting for the bacon more onion (*tarte à l'oignon*), any cooked flaky white fish, or a vegetable like asparagus or chopped broccoli. Serves 4.

*1 shortcrust pastry case, bought
    from the boulangerie,
    bought frozen from the super-
    market, or, of course, home-
    made!*
2 eggs
1 onion, thinly sliced

*50 g/2 oz gruyère cheese, roughly
    grated*
*4 rashers of streaky bacon, coarsely
    chopped*
1 small carton crème fraiche
    *(¹/₄ litre/¹/₂ pint) – 4 petit Suisse
    and a little milk is a good
    alternative*

Make the pastry or roll out the unfrozen pastry and line a medium baking tin or dish. Prick the pastry with a fork, smooth a sheet of aluminium foil over it to hold its shape when cooking, and bake in a moderate oven for 10 minutes. (It is better to cook it at this stage, as this ensures the bottom of the pastry is not soggy.)

Break the eggs into a bowl, add the cheese, cream (or milk and petit Suisse), salt and pepper and whisk together.

Melt the butter in a pan. Gently soften the onions and fry the bacon. Still whisking the mixture, pour the hot onions and bacon into it and continue until thoroughly mixed. (This ensures a light fluffy dish.)

Remove the aluminium foil and pour the mixture into the pastry case. Return to the oven and bake for 15 to 20 minutes (if the case is cooked or part cooked), or 20 to 25 minutes (if case is uncooked).

Serve hot or cold.

Croque monsieur Toasted cheese and ham sandwich

Sold in every French café, this useful snack is ideal for a light lunch. For each person

2 slices bread
butter

1 slice gruyère cheese
1 slice cooked ham

Cut the crusts off the bread and spread thinly with butter. Make a sandwich with the ham and cheese, pressing the top down firmly.

Heat more butter in a pan and fry the sandwich gently until golden on both sides. Serve immediately.

Oeufs Florentines   Eggs Florentine

A truly French dish, despite its fine Italian name! Enough for 4.

1 kg/2 lb spinach   *1 tablespoon of butter*
4 eggs   *a little lemon juice*

Wash the spinach. (The easiest way is to swirl it vigorously in a large bowl of cold water and fish the leaves out one by one.) Put it in a large saucepan with lemon juice but no water (the drops clinging to the leaves are enough). Cover the saucepan and boil for 8 to 10 minutes until the spinach is reduced to a pulp. Cut up the spinach with a knife in the saucepan then drain well. Transfer to an oven dish and make 4 'nests' in the spinach.

Break an egg into each nest and bake in a moderate oven for 5 minutes. (The baking dries out the spinach and cooks the eggs.) Serve straight from the dish with fresh-ground pepper.

Artichauts   Artichokes

One of the great delights of France, indeed the whole of Europe, is the quantity and quality of the artichoke. It can be served peeled, either as a vegetable, cold with vinaigrette, or as a starter with all its leaves.

To cook the vegetable
Cut off the stem below the 'globe'; trim the spiny points with a sharp knife or scissors; pull open the top leaves to expose the hairy 'choke' and scrape away the hairs with a spoon to expose the heart. Fill a very large saucepan with water and add a liberal amount of salt. Put the artichokes into the cold water and bring to the boil. Cook for 15 to 20 minutes and drain.

The remaining leaves will fall off, leaving the heart. Serve hot as a vegetable or cold with vinaigrette.

To cook as a starter (1 medium to large artichoke per person)
Cut off the stem below the 'globe'. Cook in boiling salted water for 40 to 45 minutes. Drain upside down. Serve hot with melted butter.

To eat pull off each leaf and dip the edible base in the butter scraping off the flesh between the teeth. Don't forget a large bowl for the discarded leaves. When down to the 'choke' cut it out carefully then eat the heart with a knife and fork.

Asperges   Asparagus

Those on holiday in the summer will, sadly, miss the asparagus season – although you may catch the tail end if you are lucky. Allow about 6 pieces per person, depending on their gluttony!

Chop off the woody white bases of the stems and tie up in a bundle. Place upright in a large saucepan and fill with water just below the green tips. Salt liberally. Boil for 10 to 14 minutes.

   Serve hot with melted butter or cold with mayonnaise or vinaigrette.

Avocat   Avocado

Unique in texture and taste, this is an easy starter or a useful addition to any salad. Allow 1 avocado for 2 people.

Just before serving cut the avocado in two lengthways and remove the large stone. A little lemon juice adds to the flavour and stops discolouration. Serve with vinaigrette or mayonnaise (page 203); fresh prawns or shrimps make an exotic variation.

Carottes au Vichy   Carrots cooked in Vichy water

A novel way of cooking carrots.

½ kg/1 lb carrots
1 tablespoon butter

½ bottle Vichy water

Wash and chop the carrots fairly small – about 1 cm/½ in. pieces. Put into a small saucepan with the butter and cover with the Vichy. Bring to the boil and simmer uncovered until all the water has evaporated, leaving the carrots cooked and glazed with butter.

Ratatouille   Mediterranean vegetable stew

This versatile dish can be eaten on its own, as a starter or as a light main course (either hot or cold), or as a vegetable with roasts or sausages. For those not given to cooking, it can be bought ready made in the *charcuterie* – but it will not compare with your own fresh dish!

These quantities feed 8, but as it reheats well and can also be eaten cold, it is best to make a good-sized pot.

3 large aubergines
3 large courgettes
3 medium onions, thinly sliced
3 large sweet peppers (preferably
  red), seeded and thinly sliced

4 cloves garlic, chopped
4 good tomatoes, chopped
parsley, finely chopped
8 tablespoons olive oil

Cut the aubergines in half lengthways, then slice thinly downwards. Slice the courgettes in the same way. Place them in a bowl, and add salt to sweat out the moisture. Leave for about 1 hour, then squeeze out moisture by hand and dry them on a cloth.

Heat the oil in a large pan and cook the onions until they are soft. Add aubergines, courgettes, peppers and garlic. Season with salt and pepper.

Cover the pan and simmer gently for 40 minutes. Add chopped tomatoes and parsley, then cook for a further 30 minutes when the vegetables will be soft but not reduced to a pulp.

Sprinkle a little parsley on top and serve hot or cold.

Moules marinières   Mussels

There are many exotic ways of preparing mussels but I consider the simplest the best. This recipe allows the fine flavour of the mussels to come through uncluttered by superfluous sauces. Serves 4.

3¹/₂ measures (6 pints) mussels
4 wineglasses white wine or cider

chopped parsley

Place mussels in a large bowl of cold water as soon as you get them to your kitchen. Sprinkle salt on top and cover until you are ready to clean them.

To clean, take a sharp knife and remove the 'beard', any barnacles or other encrustation latching on to the shell. Scrub the shells thoroughly – a painstaking job but necessary to ensure a grit-free sauce. Wash and scrub several times (changing the water each time) until the water is sand-free.

To cook, put the wine or cider into a large, heavy pan with all the mussels. Heat fast until all the shells are open. Remove those that have not opened and throw away. Transfer those that *have* opened to a large serving bowl.

Strain the liquid and return to the pan. Add chopped parsley and heat through.

Pour liquid over the mussels. Serve with plenty of fresh bread in soup plates, with a bowl for the empty shells.

Denté farci aux thym   Stuffed dentex with thyme

This recipe will do equally well for all the 'superior' larger fish, like sea bream, grey mullet, sea bass, etc. It should really be served with a flaming sprig of thyme – but to my mind this is an optional extra! Serves 4.

1 large dentex or similar (about 1 kg/2¼ lb, or a little bigger)
2 tablespoons of French mustard (preferably tarragon mustard)
1 large tomato, sliced
1 small onion, sliced

sprig wild thyme (if unavailable use dried thyme or other herb)
2 wooden toothpicks
4 tablespoons olive oil
dried or fresh herbs
juice of half a lemon

Gut, scale and wash the fish. Make three deep slanting incisions along each side. Paint the cuts and inside of the fish with the mustard. Insert some slices of tomato and onion in the cuts. Fill the inside with the remaining tomato and onion and the sprig of thyme, and secure with the toothpicks. Mix the olive oil, herbs and lemon juice. Sprinkle the fish generously with the olive oil mixture, salt and pepper.

The French grill the fish, basting it in oil, but I think it is better wrapped in aluminium foil and cooked in a moderate oven for about 35 minutes or until the flesh comes away easily from the bone. This keeps the mustard intact. If you are brave, serve with a sprig of flaming wild thyme, with potatoes or on a bed of rice.

Merlan en raïto   Whiting in a red wine sauce

This recipe can be applied to any round white fish that is large enough to be cut up. Serves 4.

1 large whiting (about 1 kg/2¹/₄ lb
*   or a little larger)*
a little flour

3 tablespoons olive oil
capers (if available)

Sauce raïto
2 tablespoons olive oil
1 onion, finely chopped
2 tablespoons flour
¹/₂ litre/1 pint red wine

boiling water
bouquet garni *(bought in a bag)*
2 cloves garlic
1 tablespoon tomato purée

Have the fish cut into steaks 2 cm/1 in. thick by the fishmonger. Heat 3 tablespoons of oil in a heavy pan. Flour the steaks. Fry quickly until cooked – perhaps 4 minutes on each side – and remove.

To make the sauce, heat the 2 tablespoons olive oil in the pan. Add chopped onions and cook until soft brown. Sprinkle flour over onions, stirring them all in. Allow to cook for 1 minute, then stir in wine and almost the same quantity of boiling water (added very slowly). Bring to the boil. Add *bouquet garni*, garlic, tomato purée and season with salt and pepper, then cook until the mixture has thickened. Remove the *bouquet garni* and the cloves of garlic.

Add the cooked fish and simmer for about 10 minutes.

Serve with rice.

Truite   Trout

Trout can be grilled with great success, cooked *à la meunière* (in butter), or this way, which is very quick and simple. For 4.

4 trout, cleaned and gutted
8 tablespoons olive oil

scant teaspoon vinegar (wine or
*   tarragon)*
sprig of thyme or other delicate herb

Heat largest pan available and add vinegar. When the pan is really hot add the oil and three wineglassfuls of water. Allow it to boil very fast until the water has nearly evaporated. Add plenty of pepper, then carefully place the fish in the fast-boiling liquid. Cover the pan and allow fish to cook for 1 minute, then reduce heat so it simmers gently for a further 3 minutes.

Serve immediately with potatoes or a salad.

Calmar farci   Stuffed squid

This recipe, which can also be used for cuttlefish, comes from the Mediterranean coast in the south-west corner of France. Serves 4.

1 large squid, 750 g/1¹/₂ lb
8 tablespoons olive oil
1 medium onion, chopped
2 carrots, thinly sliced
4 wooden toothpicks

stuffing
100 g/4 oz minced veal
100 g/4 oz minced pork
1 onion, finely chopped
parsley
1 egg yolk

Prepare squid (page 14).

Mix veal, pork, onion and parsley together in a bowl. Bind together with the yolk of egg and season with salt and pepper.

Place stuffing carefully inside the washed squid. Close with toothpicks.

Heat oil in a casserole (heavy saucepan or frying pan with a lid will do) and brown onions. Add water (enough to ensure that the squid will be completely immersed when added) and bring to the boil. Lower squid carefully into the water with the carrots. Cover and simmer very gently for 1–1½ hours.

Serve with rice.

Harengs Bretons   Brittany herrings

A recipe that combines the best products of Brittany – herrings, cider, butter and apples. Serves 4.

75 g/3 oz butter
3 dessert apples, cored and peeled
1 small onion, thinly sliced
3 sticks celery, chopped
600 ml/1¹/₂ pint dry cider

4 large herrings, cleaned and with
*   heads off*
a little flour
chopped parsley to garnish

Take your largest frying pan and melt a third of the butter. Chop up 2 of the apples and cook slowly for 10 minutes with the onion and celery. Pour over the cider, sprinkle with salt and pepper to taste, and cook for a further 10 minutes, uncovered, stirring occasionally. Put this purée mixture in a serving dish and keep hot.

Melt remaining butter in pan. Slice remaining apple and fry for about 3 minutes on each side. Remove and keep hot.

Roll the herrings in seasoned flour and fry gently – about 5 minutes on each side.

Serve herrings on cider mixture garnished with apple rings and parsley.

Harengs grillés, sauce moutarde   Grilled herrings with mustard sauce

Any strong-flavoured oily fish, such as mackerel, sardines, or bonito can be substituted for the herrings. Serves 4.

4 large herrings
oil, herbs and lemon mixture (page 12)
sauce
2 teaspoons yellow Dijon mustard   *75 g/3 oz butter, barely melted*
1 tablespoon parsley, chopped   *juice of ¹/₂ lemon*

Grill the herrings (page 12). If you do not have a barbeque, cook them in exactly the same way under the grill in the kitchen.

While herrings are cooking, make the sauce as follows: put the mustard into a bowl and stir in the chopped parsley. Add the barely melted butter and stir gently until smooth. Stir in lemon juice.

Serve the grilled herrings piping hot, topped with sauce.

Colin à l'Indienne   Curried hake

Even if your holiday diet is becoming too 'fishy' this is an interesting variation for cooking a common but wholesome fish. Serves 4.

4 tablespoons olive oil   *3 wineglasses white wine*
2 onions, thinly sliced   *2 tablespoons curry powder*
1 clove garlic, crushed   *thyme*
1 tablespoon parsley, chopped   *small (150 ml) carton* crème
4 hake steaks 3 cm/¹/₄ in. thick   *fraiche*
4 g/1¹/₂ oz butter   *juice of 1 lemon*

Heat the oil in a frying pan and soften the onion and garlic. Place in an oven dish and sprinkle with the chopped parsley. Arrange fish steaks on top, and dot each steak with a knob of butter. Mix wine, curry powder and thyme and pour over the fish.

Bake in a fairly hot pre-heated oven for 10 minutes. Add cream, salt and pepper and cook for a further 10 minutes.

Serve sprinkled with lemon juice on a bed of rice.

Rougets aux feuilles de vigne   Red mullet cooked in vine leaves

A novel way of cooking any small fish with excellent results. Ask the fishmonger or greengrocer for the vine leaves; leaves you pick at the roadside will almost certainly have been sprayed with copper sulphate, which is not poisonous but spoils the delicate flavour of the red mullet. Serves 4.

4 red mullet, gutted, scaled and
   washed
4 large vine leaves

olive oil, herb and lemon mixture
   (page 12)

When gutting the red mullet, make sure the liver is left in. Cut the red mullet along the back so open on both sides.

Dip the vine leaves in boiling water to soften – this takes about a minute.

Paint each fish with the olive oil mixture, and sprinkle with salt and pepper. Wrap up each fish, place in an oven dish and sprinkle with more olive oil mixture.

Cook in a moderate oven for 20 minutes.

Serve in the leaves, which in this recipe should not be eaten.

Rouget à la Nicoise   Red mullet in the style of Nice

This is a great speciality of the south of France. Its taste belies the ease of preparation and the cheapness of the ingredients. Serves 4.

4 tablespoons olive oil
4 large (or 8 small) red mullet
1 medium onion, chopped
2 cloves garlic, chopped
parsley, chopped
4 tomatoes, chopped

1 teaspoon tomato purée
thyme or other fresh herb
1 glass white wine
8 black olives
slices of lemon

Heat half the olive oil in a thick pan and fry the red mullet until they are stiff but not cooked through. Remove from pan.

Add the rest of the olive oil to the pan and heat. Add the chopped onion, garlic and parsley and fry until soft brown. Add the chopped tomatoes, tomato purée and thyme, season with salt and pepper. Stir the mixture well and cook for 15 minutes.

Add the white wine and olives and stir in. Place the red mullet in the sauce. Cover and simmer for a further 10 minutes.

Serve in the sauce with a slice of lemon on each fish.

Poulet à l'estragon   Tarragon chicken

Tarragon is the traditional herb for chicken. This recipe sounds difficult but is actually very simple to make. Serves 6.

75 g/3 oz butter	*3 thick slices white bread*
2 tablespoons fresh tarragon,	*1 chicken, about 1¹/₂ kg/3¹/₂ lb,*
chopped (or 1 tablespoonful if dried)	*cleaned and dressed*

Put the butter in a warmed mixing bowl and add the tarragon. Cut off the crusts of bread and crumble into the bowl. Add a little pepper and salt. Work the bread and tarragon into the butter with your fingers. Take the chicken and ease the skin away from the breast on both sides by working your fingers in from the back end of the bird. Take great care not to break the skin. Flatten half the bread mixture and work it under the skin so that it covers all the breast. Repeat on the other side. The stuffing forms a 'heat shield' so that the legs and breast are cooked at the same time and the breast is really impregnated with the tarragon butter. Rub a little more butter on the outside of the chicken and sprinkle with salt.

Bake in a moderate oven for 45 minutes per kilo plus 20 minutes over (20 minutes per pound plus 20 minutes over), basting occasionally.

Serve hot or cold.

Coq au vin   Chicken cooked in red wine

Like so many well known dishes *coq au vin* suffers from inferior imitations. Here is a true recipe that is well worth the apparent trouble in preparation. This is enough for 4 very good servings.

fresh chicken, about	*2 cloves garlic, crushed*
1¹/₄ kg/2¹/₂–3 lb with giblets	*150 g/4 oz button mushrooms*
1 carrot, thinly sliced	*150 g/4 oz salt pork cut into small*
1 onion, chopped	*cubes*
bouquet garni *(from the*	*2 tablespoons olive oil*
épicerie), or a bay leaf and a	*12 small onions (like those used for*
sprig of thyme	*pickling)*
1 bottle of good red Burgundy	*1 small glass of brandy*
(A C, or a good V D Q S will do	*1 tablespoon flour*
– page 15)	*1 tablespoon butter*

Make some stock by gently boiling the chicken giblets, carrot, onion, the *bouquet garni* or herbs together, lightly seasoned, in about

½ pint of water for 15 minutes. Pour the wine, strained stock and garlic into a saucepan and simmer gently for about half an hour or until the liquid has reduced by half. Add the mushrooms after 25 minutes.

Meanwhile joint the chicken into four pieces and season well with salt and pepper. Strain the liquid and keep the mushrooms. In the same pan lightly fry the pork in the olive oil until golden, then add the onions. When they are brown add the chicken pieces and fry them until they too are lightly browned all over. Heat the brandy in a ladle or flat spoon, set it alight and pour evenly over the chicken. When it has burnt out pour in the wine. Cover the saucepan and simmer for around 45 minutes. While the chicken is cooking work the flour and butter together and cut into small cubes. After 40 minutes add the mushrooms. When the chicken is cooked remove with the mushrooms and onions from the pan and place on a serving dish and keep hot. Return the pan to a low heat and add the butter–flour cubes and stir until the sauce thickens allowing it to come just, but no nearer, to the boil. Pour the sauce over the chicken and serve immediately with fried bread or toast.

Boeuf bourguignon   Beef cooked in Burgundy wine

This is an expensive dish, and although quick to prepare it takes a long time to cook. Don't economize on the wine – inferior wine will ruin an exquisite dish. Here is a simplified, and to my mind superior, recipe for 4 good servings.

1 kg/2¹/₄ lb beef (top leg crosse, top rump alayau)
100 g/4 oz salt pork (sliced hard pork sausage is a good alternative)
50 g/2 oz butter or 2 tablespoons olive oil
8 small shallots or 1 medium onion, chopped

1 tablespoon flour
¹/₂ litre good red Burgundy (preferably A C, but a V D Q S will do)
1 clove garlic
1 bouquet garni – buy one already made up from the épicerie

Cut the beef into 7 cm/2½ in. squares and the salt pork into strips. Melt the butter in a heavy pan and fry the salt pork until the fat is transparent. Remove. 'Seal' the beef in the hot butter until brown on all sides. Add shallots and cook until soft brown. Sprinkle the flour over the meat and shallots and stir until it has been taken up.

Add the wine over a low heat, stirring until well mixed with the *fécule* of flour and butter in the pan. Add the garlic, *bouquet garni* and season with salt and pepper.

Gently bring almost to the boil, then simmer on a very low heat for 2 hours, topping up with water, or preferably stock, if too thick. Add salt pork or slices of sausage and cook for another ½ hour.

Remove the clove of garlic and the *bouquet garni*. Serve and enjoy!

Côtes de porcs normandes Pork chops with a cider sauce

This recipe is a subtle blend of distinct flavours. Serves 4.

50 g/2 oz butter
4 shallots, halved, or 2 small onions, sliced
4 pork chops, preferably loin chops with kidney
1 apple, peeled, cored and thinly sliced

1 tablespoon parsley, finely chopped
1 wineglass still cider
½ teaspoonful Dijon or similar mustard

Heat the butter in a heavy pan and add the shallots. Cook until soft brown. Push to the side of the pan. Cook the pork chops and apple slices slowly, in the covered pan, turning once. Remove the chops. Stir mushy apples and onions together and add the mustard, making a thick sauce. Thin sauce with the cider and bring to the boil.

Return chops to the sauce to reheat.

Serve with a green salad or mashed potatoes.

Sorbet à l'orange et yaourt   Orange and yoghurt sorbet

A very fine iced pudding with an unusual taste and texture. Ample for 6.

6 oranges (preferably 2 navel and 4 blood oranges)
1 wineglass brandy (optional)
2×150 ml cartons plain yoghurt or 6 petit Suisse
about 50 g/2 oz sugar (quantity depending on the sweetness of the oranges and your taste)

1 tablespoon orange liqueur, such as Cointreau (optional)
1¹/₂ tablespoons gelatine
2 egg whites

Grate the rind from the 2 navel oranges. Remove the pith, cut the flesh into thin slices and either marinate in the brandy or cover and keep aside.

Squeeze the remaining oranges and strain into a bowl. Add the grated rind and yoghurt, mixing well with the sugar. Put the Cointreau together with 2 tablespoons water (3 if you omit the Cointreau) in a small pan and sprinkle the gelatine over. Warm slowly, stirring until the gelatine has dissolved. Allow to cool a little.

Add gelatine to the orange mixture, mixing them well together.

Whisk the egg whites until very stiff. Fold into the orange mixture gently.

Pour into a serving dish and freeze until solid.

Serve with the orange slices on top.

Pêches au vin blanc   Peaches in white wine

A good way to serve this delicate-flavoured but cheap fruit.

for each person
2 peaches
2 tablespoons white wine
sugar

Dip the peaches in boiling water until the skin cracks. They then peel easily.

Slice into a serving bowl and sprinkle with sugar. Pour the white wine over the fruit and chill.

Eat soon after preparation, before the fruit goes mushy.

Spain

SHOPPING

Today most foodstuffs are available all over Spain – only price separates the local produce in season from the imported. It obviously makes sense to buy the local produce cheaply, and you will find it in the local markets.

The municipal market *mercado* in Spain is often a grand building. The high domed glass roof harbours dozens of noisy sparrows, while below the large hall is divided up by clusters of stalls like old-fashioned cow-sheds.

Every day (except Sundays and public holidays) is market day, from 8 o'clock in the morning until 2 o'clock in the afternoon. The stalls are carefully laid out; banks of fresh vegetables and fruit, basketfuls of pale brown eggs and plump chickens, great sides of meat beside every kind of offal and so many salamis, sausages and cheeses hanging from the ceiling of the stall that you can hardly see the seller. In another building the fishmonger has arranged his wares artistically – *pescadillas* with their tails in their mouths, a battalion of fish on a parade-ground of ice flanked with seaweed and lemon – it seems almost shameful to buy anything and disturb his display!

The village markets are less formal. They usually take place once a week, when dozens of rattletrap vans descend on the village square and set up their trestle tables and awnings. They spread out bundles of cloth, hang up lines of clothes, lay out cheap shoes and arrange earthenware pots. This is a good place to buy *cazuelas* – the cheap earthenware dishes that are indispensable for Spanish cookery. On the other days the locals have an impromptu market, usually beside the church, selling fruit and vegetables and, if close to the sea, fish as well.

Shops seem so pale after the colour of the market. Empty too! Because of the heat the butcher in his *carnicería* often keeps the meat in the chill room and sells from a card in the window; there are dozens of Atlantic and Mediterranean fish in the fishmonger *pescadería*. Both shops are open in the morning between 9 o'clock and half past 1 or 2 o'clock, but rarely in the afternoons – perhaps a tradition left over from the days before chill rooms and refrigerators.

Other shops, like the grocer *comestible* or *calmados*, the pastry shop *pastelería*, and the breadshop *panadería*, open from 9 in the morning until 7 or 8 at night, closing for lunch and siesta between 2 and 5 o'clock. The *pastelería* is open on Sundays.

Here are a few phrases to help you on your way;

Good morning	**Buenos días**
Good afternoon	**Buenas tardes**
Please	**Por favor**
Thank you	**Gracias**
Please can I have ... kilos of ...?	**¿Por favor me da ... kilos de ...?**
That's too expensive	**Es muy caro/Es demasiado caro**
A little more please	**Un poco más por favor**
Less please	**Menos por favor**
Please will you cut it for me?	**¿Me lo puede cortar, por favor?**
Please will you clean it for me?	**¿Me lo puede limpiar, por favor?**
Please can I have some small fish for a mixed fried fish dish?	**¿Me puede dar pescado pequeño y variado para fritura, por favor?**

1	**uno**
2	**dos**
3	**tres**
4	**cuatro**
5	**cinco**
6	**seis**
7	**siete**
8	**ocho**
9	**nueve**
10	**diez**
100	**cién**
1000	**mil**
half	**medio, media**
quarter	**cuarto**

The Fishmonger   **Pescadería**

During the first triumvirate of Rome (around 60 BC) the Senate passed a law governing the sale of fish in the far-off province of Citerior, now northern Spain. The law stated: 'No fishmonger will sit down until he has sold or disposed of all his fish!' This crafty legislation guaranteed fresh fish all the time in the markets. The law, of course, has gone, but fresh fish is still the order of the day!

The fish markets are sometimes in a separate building from the main market. They generally open around 8 o'clock and finish when they have sold out. Spanish fishermen rarely go out on Sundays so there is no fresh fish on Mondays. You will see the fishmonger uses two implements to fillet: one a large knife with a deep, flat curved blade and the other a large pair of scissors.

There is an abundance of fish around the Spanish coast, and a great variety of types and species. The more common include:

anchovy	**boquerones, anchoa, bocarate** small silver green-backed fish sold either fresh, or salted or tinned at the grocers
angler fish	**rape** mostly mouth and teeth, grey–white with brown markings and black at fins. Firm flesh in tail resembles lobster
bass, sea	**lubina** silver with darker back and white stomach. Good
bonito	**bonito** very large silver–blue fish usually sold in thick steaks
bream, black	**chopa** dark grey back with golden yellow stripes on sides – excellent
bream, gilthead	**dorada** silver–grey with black spots on cheek and golden crescent between eyes
bream, red	**besugo** meaning 'angry person' silver with reddish back and black spot on shoulder
bream, sea	**pargo** silver fish with reddish tint to fins
bream, Spanish	**aligote** silver fish with enormous eyes and black spot by side fin
clams	**chirla** small, grey with smooth shells **almejas** small, red with smooth shells
cod	**bacalao, moya** not strictly cod but of the same family
cockles	**coquinas**
crab	**cangrejo**

crab, spider	**centolla** extra-long thin legs
crayfish	**langosta** like lobster, but larger and without claws
cuttlefish	**holladores** similar to squid but smaller and whiter
eels	**anguila**
	angulas tiny eel fry – expensive
eel, conger	**congrio, zafio** popular Spanish fare sold whole, or cut into steaks
hake	**merluza** big; **pescada** medium; **pescadilla** small; a dappled grey fish, very common, sold in steaks, slices or whole. Sizes vary from a few inches to a yard long
John Dory	**gallo San Pedro** flat, deep grey fish with an ugly head. Supposedly gained its name from St Peter's thumb print on its shoulder
mackerel, Atlantic	**caballa** blue–black back with dark blue lines across body
mackerel, horse	**jurel** prominent eyes and scaly striped line down side of light green–blue body. Good eating
mackerel, Spanish or chub	**estornino** spots as opposed to stripes – better eating than **caballa**
mullet, grey	**mujol** leaden blue–grey back, and pale underside – common and not expensive
	lisa a better eating variety
mullet, red	**salmonete** a bright red fish recognizable from the two barbules under its chin
mussels	**mejillones** now all cultivated
octopus	**pulpo** buy those with two rows of suckers on the tentacles
oysters	**ostras** now mostly cultivated. Go for a particularly good variety from Cadiz called **ostion** but this must not be eaten raw – fine cooked in stews
plaice	**platija** found only on the north coast
prawns	**gambas**
prawns, deep sea	**langostino** extra large fleshy prawns up to 20 cm/9 in. in length

sardines	**sardinas** green–blue back with silver sides – cheap and common. Avoid **alacha** as they are coarse
scallops	**almejones** largish purse-shaped molluscs, red in colour
	morcillón smaller with smooth shells
shrimps	**quisquillón, quisquilla** sold cooked or raw, dismissed by the Spanish as fit only for filling omelettes
skate	**raya** only 'wings' sold, in steaks
sole	**lenguado** a delicately flavoured expensive flat fish
	lenguadina a thinner version. White to pink in colour. Not as good but cheaper
	gayo an even poorer relation with definite red markings round the edges
squid	**calamares** sold either whole or cut in rings
swordfish	**pez de espada, aguja pala** large silver fish easily recognized by sword beak – sold in steaks
trout	**trucha** all artificially produced and not expensive
tunny	**atún** blue-backed silvery spindle-shaped fish, usually sold in steaks as can be very large. A good buy as little waste
turbot	**rodaballo** flat fish with brown, spotted back. Excellent eating

The Butcher   **La Carnicería**

The day's bull-fighting programme is written up in the local paper. It says who the matadors are and the weight and breeding of the bulls. More important (for the Spanish housewife), it tells from which horse-butcher *expendeduria de carne de caballo* the bulls will be sold. This meat, as the queues outside the shop seems to prove, is exceptionally good (particularly the tail), for the bulls are well fed and pampered except for the last half hour of their life!

On other days this shop only sells horsemeat; the butcher *arnicería* sells all other meat, poultry and game. Do not be put off if the shop appears to be empty, as on hot days the butcher stores everything in the chill room and advertises what is for sale in a list in the window. The cuts of all meat and game are shown in a blue diagram displayed behind the counter together with a list of the government-controlled prices.

Beef **Carne de vaca, buey**

The best beef in Spain comes from the north, where the climate and grass is ideal. In the south good beef is expensive and poor beef may be an old tough animal.

brisket	**pecho**
fillet steak	**filete**
flank	**falda**
leg of beef	**pierna**
neck	**cuello**
rump steak	**cadera**
sirloin	**solomillo**
sirloin steak	**lomo bajo**
top ribs	**costilletas**

Veal **Carne de ternera**

Spanish veal is not the delicate calf meat with milk-white flesh but comes from a much larger animal slaughtered well before it has reached maturity. The meat is tender and good value, and again the best comes from the north.

breast or belly	**pecho**
chops	**chuletas**
knuckle	**jarrete**
loin	**lomo**
scrag end of neck	**cuello**
shoulder	**espaldo**
topside	**tapa**

Pork **Carne de cerdo**

Pork is good all over Spain, particularly in the north where the pigs graze in the oak forests.

belly	**pecho**
knuckle or lower leg	**hueso de jamón**

leg of pork	**pata de cerdo**
loin	**lomo**
neck	**cuello**
shoulder or hand	**paleta**
tenderloin	**solomillo de cerdo**
trotters	**manitas**

Lamb   **Cordero**

Lamb is a good buy all over Spain, particularly where the beef is a little suspect or expensive.

best end of neck	**costilletas de primera**
breast	**pecho de cordero**
leg	**pierna de cordero**
loin chop	**chuleta de cordero**
middle neck	**costilla de segunda**
rack	**chuletas de palo**
saddle	**silla de cordero**
scrag end	**cuello**
shoulder	**paleta** or **espalda** a good buy when tied and boned ready for roasting, **paleta** or **espalda redonda en balón**

Offal   **Menudillos**

Offal is usually sold in the butcher's shop but in the larger markets special stalls sell only offal.

brains	**sesos**
calf's foot	**manos de ternera**
kidneys	**riñones**
liver	**hígado**
tongue, fresh	**lengua**
tripe	**callos**

The Poultry Shop   **La Pollería**

A 1926 menu on display in a Madrid restaurant, *Jai Allai*, shows lobster at 3 pesetas and chicken at 6. Alas, the roles are now reversed and it is the chicken that is inexpensive! Chickens are usually sold fresh still with the head, feet and innards. The *pollería* will dress them for you if asked.

Chicken	**pollo**
back	**carcasa**
body minus legs and wings	**pechuga**
breast	**filetes de pollo**
legs	**patas**
lights (heart, liver and lungs)	**higados**
wings	**alítas**

Also sold in the *pollería* is a wide range of game *caza menor*, and eggs.

duck	**pata** occasionally wild in the more remote areas, but more often bred for the table
eggs	**huevos** sold by the dozen, generally loose from a large basket
guinea hen	**gallina de Guinea** quite common in Spain, this bird (grey with white speckles) is not expensive but can be tough
hare	**liebre** quite common in the more remote parts of Spain. Choose only **lebrato**, a young hare up to 1 year old
partridge	**perdiz** a very common game bird in Spain, this red-legged, dark brown bird is quite expensive
quail	**codorniz** a tiny bird, quite common and inexpensive, which is always sold dressed for cooking. Allow two or three birds per person
rabbit	**conejo** usually sold dressed and skinned, most rabbit are wild but now a few are bred for the markets

General Store   **Comestibles**
Delicatessen   **Mantequería**

In Spain there is no clear distinction between these shops, but in general the *comestibles* are the smaller self-service supermarkets selling the cheaper range of foodstuffs, tinned and frozen, oil, wines and spirits, and bread. The *mantequería* is a much smarter shop, combining everything in the *comestibles* with all the *charcutería* products and often pastries as well. The supermarkets *supermercados* are everywhere and sell everything.

Groceries

breadcrumbs	**pan rallado**
capers	**alcaparras**
caramel	**caramelo**
cayenne pepper	**pimienta de cayenna**
chick peas	**garbanzos**
cinnamon	**canela**
cloves	**clavo de comer**
coffee	**café**
cumin seeds	**semillas de comino**
currants	**pasa de Corinto**
curry powder	**condimento con curry**
flour	**harina**
honey	**miel**
jam	**mermelada**
lentils	**lentejas**
macaroni	**macarrones**
mayonnaise	**mahonesa**
mineral water	**agua mineral**; fizzy **con gas**; or flat **sin gas**
mustard	**mostaza**
noodles	**tallarines**
nutmeg	**nuez moscada**
oil, olive	**aceite de oliva**
oil, peanut	**aceite de cacahuetes**
oil, sunflower	**aceite de girasol**
paprika	**pimenta húngara** or **pimentón**
pepper	**pimienta**
peppercorns	**granos de pimienta**
raisins	**pasas**
rice	**arroz** the long-grained **Valencian** rice is the best
saffron	**azafrán** the real saffron from crocus petals is ten times the price of gold! A powder substitute is common and inexpensive

salt	**sal**; **sal marina** sea salt
salt cod	**bacalao salado** a traditional food which is becoming less common
sugar	**azúcar**
tea	**té** a few British brands are sold (best to take your own)
vanilla	**vainilla** sold in black sticks or pods
vermicelli	**fideos**
vinegar	**vinagre**

Dairy products

butter	**mantequilla** usually unsalted
	mantequilla salada salted butter
cheese	**queso** most cheese in Spain comes from ewes' milk. There are endless varieties of local cheese, those common throughout Spain include:
	bola Holandés common cows' milk cheese similar to Dutch Edam
	manchego añejo a very hard ewes' milk cheese
	manchego en aceite like *añejo* but soaked in oil
	queso de Burgos an excellent cream cheese
	queso de nata cream cheese. **Villalón** is a good variety
margarine	**margarina**
milk	**leche** long-life milk in cartons; fresh in litre plastic bags

Charcutería

Basically *charcutería* is everything to do with the pig once it has ceased to be fresh pork. Like every other foodstuff in Spain, it has strong regional variations to suit the local style of cooking.

bacon	**panceta** like salt pork and not comparable to British bacon, as usually very fatty and comes from the belly. Sold in slabs, although it can be sliced into rashers
	bacón higher quality, like British bacon

brawn	**chicharrones**
fat	**tocino** sold by the kilo
ham	**jamón**; **jamón asado** boiled without bone; **jamón serrano legítimo** salt cured (like Italian *prosciutto*); **jamón de jabugo** ham cured in the snow, is very expensive but excellent; **jamón York** York ham, boned and unsalted
sausages	Spanish sausages are made from lean pork, fat, pepper and garlic, and eaten raw, or made from lean beef and pork, fat and spices for cooking in stews. The most common varieties include:
	butifarra fat pork seasoned with cloves, pepper, nutmeg and white wine
	chorizo very spicy and peppery dried sausage, usually red in colour
	longaniza blanca lean pork, marjoram, white wine and salt
	morcilla like black pudding, blood mixed with pork fat, onion, marjoram and pepper. Differs in each region
	morcilla blanca chicken, fat bacon, eggs, parsley and spices
	mortadela lean pork, spices and salt
	salchichas fillet of veal and pork, white pepper and rum. Fresh sausages are sometimes not made when weather is hot
	salchichón fresh pork sausage made from fillet pork, bacon and white pepper. Again may not be made in the summer when it is too hot
	sobrasada a spicey dried sausage from Mallorca
spare ribs	**casullas adobadas** sold with highly spiced sauce

The Bakery   **La Panadería**

There is a *panadería* even in the smallest village. They open early in time for breakfast at around 7 o'clock, and stay open until they have sold out. Some open again between 5 and 8 o'clock in the evening. The baker *el panadero* bakes every day except Sundays, so bread *pan* is always fresh. It is sold at government-controlled prices by the piece, and comes in many shapes and sizes. Also sold in the *panadería* are the many sweet breakfast rolls and cakes.

bread	**pan** every region has its own special type and shape of bread. Those that are common all over Spain include:
	bambas large soft rolls
	bombolinos round soft baps
	pan bombón a small round soft loaf
	pan corriente or **pan flama** a long fattish crusty loaf with diagonal cuts on top
	pan de molde soft sliced bread
	pan gallego a round soft loaf with a single score down the middle
	pan pequeño very small crusty loaf like the **pan flama**
	rosquillas small or large crusty bread rings
	pan tamil long, thin, hard *batons*
brioche	**medias noches** a very typical Spanish breakfast 'cake', cup-shaped and made from a yeast dough
	ensaimada similar but spiral shaped
	trenzas figure of eight shape and dusted with sugar
croissant	**croissant** a puff-pastry crescent-shaped breakfast roll, sometimes sugared

The Pastry Shop **La Pastelería**

The larger the breadshop *panadería* the more likely it is to include a *pastelería*. Certainly all pastries, cakes and biscuits can be bought in the *mantequería* together with the many savouries.

The Spanish, with their sweet tooth, have a vast selection of cakes, pastries and biscuits that vary from region to region.

biscuits	**galletas** collective name for all proprietary brands of biscuits bought in packets
	pastas small, round, flat and yellow

Tortetes

Palmeros

Truffas

Palos Crema

Rosquillas

Huesos

Pastas

Pastries

cakes	**pasteles** cakes are usually sponge dressed with cream
	magdalenas little cakes covered with cream
	pasteles de moka coffee cake
doughnuts	**rosquillas**
éclairs	**palos crema** either plain or with chocolate
mille-feuilles	**suelos** flaky pastry with cream and jam
pastries	**palmeros** heart-shaped flaky pastry covered with chocolate and/or nuts
	empanadas rather greasy but very sweet pastry
savouries	**tarta** either empty shortcrust pastry cases or already filled with either fish or meat
truffles	**truffas** rich chocolate ball covered with cocoa.

A sweet which is very common in all of Spain but has no equivalent in English is **huevo hilado**. It is very sweet, yellow in colour and looks rather like Shredded Wheat but is in fact spun egg whites and sugar.

The Greengrocer   **La Verdulería**

One of the great advantages of Spain is the abundance, general cheapness and variety of fresh vegetables and fruit. Everything is sold by the kilo except for herbs that come by the bunch.

artichoke	**alcachofa** shaped like a globe with tough overlapping scaly green leaves. They can be eaten raw when young, tender and purple in colour; or cooked when larger
asparagus	**espárrago** sold by the bundle, these light green shoots with purple–green heads are fairly inexpensive in their spring season. Wild asparagus is smaller and greener and often used in *tortillas*
aubergines or egg plants	**berenjenas** large, oval shaped and deep purple colour
avocado	**aguacate** either purple or green. Both have a light green waxy flesh and are pear shaped. Ripe avocados give a little when pressed on the stalk end
basil	**albahaca** excellent leaf herb sold by the bunch
bay leaf	**laurel** sold, sometimes given away, by the bunch
beans, broad	**habas**
beans, runner	**judías verdes, vainas**
beetroot	**remolacha** common throughout the year
blette	**acelgas** similar to spinach but with thicker, edible stalks and smaller leaf
Brussels sprouts	**coles de Bruselas**

cabbage	**col** similar to the British hard white cabbage
	berza loose-leafed cabbage
	lombarda red cabbage
carrots	**zanahorias**
cauliflower	**coliflor** common vegetable with a long season
celery	**apio**
chicory	**endivía** greenish-white close-leaved salad vegetable, slightly bitter taste
chives	**cebolletas** sold or given away in bunches
courgettes	**calabacines** baby marrows that are best when not more than 15 cm/6 in. long. They are sometimes sold with their edible flowers
cucumbers	**pepinos**
endive	**escarola** similar to a lettuce, with thick curly leaves and a slightly bitter taste
fennel	**hinojo** the swollen stem of an aromatic plant, it is pale green to white in colour with a strong aniseed flavour. Avoid any that are dark green
garlic	**ajo** sold by the head *cabeza*, essential to Spanish cookery
kale or spring greens	**berzas**
leeks	**puerros**
lettuce	**lechuga**
marjoram	**mejorana** the most common Spanish herb, sold by the bundle
mint	**hierbabuena** fairly common herb, sold by the bunch
mushrooms	**champiñones** cultivated mushrooms sold the year round. The expensive wild mushrooms **seta** in spring only
olives	**aceitunas** either black, pickled ripe in olive oil, or green, pickled unripe in brine and garlic
onions	**cebollas** the original Spanish onion!
	cebolletas spring onions
oregano	**orégano** sold fresh by the bunch or dried

parsley	**perejil** many varieties. Most common has long stalks and wide-serrated leaves
peas	**guisantes**
peppers	**pimientos** the larger are better for stuffing, the smaller are stronger-tasting and better for flavouring and frying. They are either red **pimientos morrones**, green **pimientos verdes** or dried **pimientos secos**
potatoes	**patatas**
pumpkin	**calabaza** large orange-fleshed gourds, mostly from the south of Spain. They are sold in pieces by the kilo
radishes	**rábanos** sold by the bunch
rosemary	**romero** a common herb sold by the bunch or given away
sage	**salvia** sold by the bunch
shallots	**chalotes** very strong small onions
spinach	**espinaca** a common vegetable sold most of the year round
thyme	**tomillo** sold fresh by the bunch, it is widely used in Spanish cookery
tomatoes	**tomates** either red or green (the colour is immaterial), they are found everywhere, usually large enough for stuffing
turnips	**nabos** white in colour, either long and thin or round
watercress	**berros de arroyo** slightly larger leaf than British varieties but the taste and use are the same

The Fruiterer   **La Frutería**

In Spain the fruit in season is sold literally everywhere – on the roadside, from private houses and of course in the shops and markets. There is always a wide choice – even in winter, when fruit is imported from the Canary Islands.

almonds	**almendras** fresh almonds are cheap and plentiful. Essential to Spanish cookery and sold between May and Christmas

Fruit & Vegetables

apples	**manzanas** plentiful and inexpensive. The best varieties are the golden **gran esmit** and **reineta**
bananas	**plátanos** mostly imported from the Canaries, but a few are grown in southern Spain
apricots	**albaricoques** a delicious late summer fruit, it is plentiful and inexpensive in season
cherries	**cerezas**
chestnuts	**castañas** common and inexpensive in their late autumn season
coconut	**coco** quite common and widely used in confectionery
dates	**dátiles**
figs	**higos** very common, cheap and plentiful from late summer onwards
grapefruit	**pomelo** sold individually but charged by the kilo

grapes	**uvas** dessert grapes are cheap and plentiful and either black **negras** or light green **blancas**. **Moscateles** muscatel grapes are sweet, green and good
greengages	**ciruelas verdales** light green–yellow plum, a fine, juicy summer fruit
hazel nuts	**avellanas** very common in the autumn
lemons	**limónes** cheap and plentiful throughout the year; medium ones are the best buy
medlars or loquats	**nísperos** small but succulent, orange-skinned fruit, sometimes with brown blotches, the orange flesh has two or three large pips. Good eating and cheap
melon	**melón** many varieties, all inexpensive, are sold by the piece *uno*, but charged by the kilo
melon, water	**sandía** enormous fruit with dark green skin, bright red flesh and black pips
oranges	**naranjas** either those for eating, the **Washington** with a small hole on top with a 'crazed' button poking through, or the smaller varieties for pressing, they are both abundant and inexpensive
peaches	**melocotónes** excellent and plentiful throughout the summer
pears	**peras** the most common variety is **pera de Roma**; water pears **pera de agua** are delicious and refreshing – worth the extra expense
pineapple	**piña** mostly imported they are sold individually *por una*
plums	**ciruelas** excellent first-season fruit, cheap and plentiful
prickly pears	**higos chumbos** the fruit of a cactus, sold mostly in the south from the roadside. It is better to let the vendor peel it as the succulent yellow fruit is covered with sharp spikes
raspberries	**frambuesas** delicious but expensive

strawberries	**fresones** quite common in season and fairly cheap except for the wild strawberries **fresas**
walnuts	**nuez de nogal** expensive outside their autumn season

Wines and Spirits

Wines

Spain may be short of water but never wine. Even when all Europe's vineyards were decimated by disease in the nineteenth century the British consul reported that wine was being used to mix cement during a drought! The constant hot sun raises the sugar content in the grape, which in turn makes the wine sweeter and higher in alcohol content – so envy the Spaniards, none of whom would think of sitting down to a meal without a bottle of wine – usually the *vino corriente* (cheap wine). It is sold either at the *comestibles* already bottled, or, if you are lucky, at the *bodega* (the wine shop) out of an enormous barrel.

A visit to the *bodega* is an experience. You should take along your own bottles for filling – corks are provided free. Chalked on the barrels is the wine type – either *tinto* (red), *clarete* (a less strong red), *blanco* (white) and sometimes *vino rancio* ('old' wine – strong, usually white, to be drunk as an aperitif). Beside the names is the strength in degrees proof and the price per litre. Do not be afraid to ask to try the wine – it is expected.

The bottled wines *vinos de marla* or *vinos embotellados* cannot really be compared with French vintages, although there are fine exceptions like those from the north in the Rioja region around Logroño where the climate and soil are ideal for the production of excellent wines like those from the *Bodegas Bilbainas* and *CUNE*. Look out for other good names like *La Rioja Alta*, *Marqués de Murrieta*, and *Bodegas Berberana*. Another area for better wine is Penédes in Catalonia which produces all the *Torres* wines.

Vintage wines can be recognized by word *cosecha*, and the year of the vintage on the label. The *año* denotes the number of years the wine has been aged in the cask before bottling – thus 4° *año* has been aged for four years before bottling. To the Spanish the longer the better.

Some of the hundreds of other bottled Spanish wines are as follows.

Champagne, since it is not from the Champagne region of France, can no longer be allowed to be called Champagne although it is made in exactly the same way. Spanish 'champagne' tends to be rather sweet unless you buy *bruto*; Casa Codornio produce a fine *Bruto*.

Chacoli from the Basque region is a *vino verde* (a young wine). Usually white, it is crisp and refreshing.

Montilla a white wine from the Cordoba area of Andalusia. Light and dry, usually drunk as an aperitif, it has the same types as sherry – *fino*, *amontillado* and *oloroso*.

Valdepeñas Valdepeñas is a town in the centre of the wide open plateau of La Mancha in New Castille – probably the largest wine-growing area in Spain. A lot of the wine goes for blending but is good when drunk as *vino corriente* actually in the district.

Sherry   **Jerez**

Sherry, popular in England since it was first imported in the sixteenth century, comes from one particular area in the south – Jerez de la Frontera – from which it takes its name. It is made by blending the special wine from the area and is allowed to ferment and mature under the most controlled conditions and care. The hundreds of makes of sherry all fall within these specifications:

amontillado light and dry, amber in colour with a pungent aroma and nut-like flavour

fino very dry, pale topaz colour

manzanilla comes from Sanlucar de Barrameda, where the sea breezes from the Atlantic are said to cause its aromatic dry quality

moscatel sweet desert wine named after its grape. Used in blending sweet or cream sherries

oloroso dark gold, almost reddish-brown with a strong bouquet. Basically dry, it leaves an aftertaste of sweetness

Brandy **Coñac**

Spanish brandy is good, so long as you do not try to compare it to the French *cognac*. It has its own distinct flavour. The better-known varieties in the cheaper range are *Fundador*, *Osborne* and *Soberano*, while *Magno* is finer and correspondingly more expensive.

COOKING

Generally speaking Spanish cooking is like Spanish weather – in the north you stew, in the middle you roast and in the south you fry!

Like all countries the Spanish cuisine varies regionally – influenced by the local ingredients and by-gone invaders like the Romans, Moors and Celts.

Apart from the ubiquitous *paella* Spanish cooking is uncomplicated, depending for its flavour on the quality of the ingredients, the timing of cooking and the selection of seasoning. Olive oil forms the basis of traditional Spanish cooking, just as garlic, onions and tomatoes are the basic ingredients for most of their sauces. Seasoning is subtle – parsley is used a great deal, so is ham, or just the tip of a bay leaf, a sprig of thyme, or ten crushed almonds.

The Spanish need plenty of recipes as they never stop eating! Breakfast *desayuno* is followed by a mid-morning nibble *almuerzo* of something like an omelette, or a chop or two with bread and wine. The main meal of the day *comida* comes at 2 o'clock and can be anything up to 5 courses. In case you are a little peckish around 6 *merienda* is a cup of coffee and a cake, while dinner *cena* is much later at 10 o'clock; and if guests are present it is another heavy meal. Do not try to emulate the Spanish, particularly eating a heavy *paella* late at night.

Gazpacho   Cold soup

This traditional Spanish soup from Andalusia is cold and delicious. It is particularly refreshing for lunch, or dinner on a hot evening. Serves 4.

3 medium onions	*8 tablespoons olive oil*
3 slices white bread (preferably slightly stale)	*24 almonds, blanched and peeled*
	1 teaspoon cumin seeds
2 × 400 g cans tinned tomatoes	*2 tablespoons wine vinegar*

Chop the onions very finely. Crumble the bread and place in bowl with chopped onions. (Or pass onions through a mincer followed by the bread.) Add the tinned tomatoes and stir, breaking up the whole tomatoes. Add the oil and stir until the soup becomes creamy.

Crush almonds and cumin seeds (the back of a wooden spoon against a chopping board will do). Make into a thin paste with a little water and the vinegar, then add to the soup, stirring in well.

Sieve the soup, or liquidize in an electric blender.

Thin the soup with iced water if the *gazpacho* is too thick – though it should be thickish in consistency. Cool with ice cubes before serving.

Sopa de uvas blancas de Russo   Cold grape soup in the style of Russo

An unusual blend of very different flavours – grapes and garlic – that to my taste works well. Serves 4.

1 or 2 cloves garlic
24 almonds, blanched and peeled
1 tablespoon olive oil
1 tablespoon vinegar

2 slices white bread
ice cubes
small bunch white grapes

Crush the garlic and almonds with a little salt (the back of a wooden spoon against a chopping board will do). Put into a bowl. Stir in the olive oil, making a paste, then add the vinegar.

Remove the crusts from the bread, then crumble into a soup bowl and add ½ litre/1 pint cold water. When mushy add the almond paste and stir thoroughly. Throw in the ice cubes and refrigerate for at least an hour.

Peel and pip the grapes, placing 5 or 6 in each soup bowl.

Thin the soup with iced water before serving if it is too thick.

Tortilla española   Potato omelette

Tortillas are synonymous with Spain. They are eaten everywhere, hot and cold. This recipe is for the true tortilla – all others are sham! This is enough for 2 good-sized portions or a starter for 4.

½ kg/1 lb potatoes
1 large onion

4 tablespoons olive oil
6 eggs

Peel the potatoes and onions. Slice both thinly.

Heat most of the oil in a heavy pan then add the potatoes, onions and salt. Cook gently until golden brown but not crisp.

Whisk the eggs in a bowl with a little salt and pepper. Quickly transfer the potatoes, onion and a little of the oil to the egg mixture and mix well.

Heat the pan, adding or pouring off oil so that the pan is lightly oiled. Pour in the mixture, shaking the pan all the time to stop it sticking to the bottom. Cook for 2–3 minutes until firm. Remove from heat and turn upside-down on to a plate.

Heat a little more oil in the pan and slide the tortilla back into the pan – the cooked side up. (Small ones can be turned with a slice but this one is too big.) Cook for another 2–3 minutes to allow second side to cook.

Serve with a green salad or cold, cut in slices like a cake.

Huevos a la flamenca   Eggs flamenca

This bright red dish is aptly named as it evokes all the colours of a Spanish sunset! Typically Spanish, it is served to each person in an individual *cazuela* earthenware pot. These quantities make enough for 4.

4 tablespoons olive oil
4 medium onions, chopped
100 g/4 oz ham, chopped
6 tomatoes, sliced
4 sweet peppers, the small hot
  variety (pimientos), *sliced*

200 g/8 oz chorizo, *sliced thinly*
500 g/1 lb cooked peas or fresh beans
8 eggs
4 tablespoons parsley, chopped

Heat the oil in a pan. Add onions and ham and cook for 2–3 minutes. Add tomatoes and half the peppers and cook for a few more minutes, until soft.

Meanwhile arrange the sliced *chorizo* around the edges of four *cazuelas*.

Preheat the oven to hot. Add peas or beans to the cooked mixture, stir, then divide the mixture between the *cazuelas*. Break two eggs in the middle of each and cook in the oven until the white of the eggs sets, leaving the yolks soft. Sprinkle with chopped parsley and garnish with the remaining strips of red pepper.

Serve at once in the *cazuelas*.

Berenjenas rellenas Stuffed aubergines

How fortunate the Mediterranean countries are with their plentiful supply of exotic, cheap vegetables and the endless ways of preparing them. Here is a good example. Hot or cold, it serves 4 as a starter, 2 as a main course.

a little lemon juice
1 wine glass milk
1 slice bread
2 largish aubergines
3 tablespoons olive oil
1 onion, sliced

1 tomato, chopped
100 g/4 oz ham, chopped
2 tablespoons parsley, chopped
50 g/scant 2 oz cheese (such as
    queso arrego), *finely grated*

Add the lemon juice to the milk and soak bread in this liquid.

Boil aubergines whole for 5 minutes. Cut in half lengthways and scoop out the flesh, taking care not to damage the skins. Chop the flesh coarsely. Heat the oil in a pan, cook the aubergine flesh and onion until just tender, and add the tomato.

Squeeze out the bread and discard the liquid. Add the onions, tomato and aubergine from the pan, then the ham, parsley and cheese. Season with salt and pepper. Work in together with your fingers so it is well mixed but not stodgy.

Fill the skins and place in an oven-proof dish. Bake for 45 minutes in a moderate oven.

Serve hot or cold.

Espinacas con pasas y piñones Spinach with raisins and pine-nuts

A useful recipe for spinach, to serve hot as a vegetable or cold as a salad. Enough for 4.

1 kg/2¼ lb spinach
a little lemon juice
2 tablespoons olive oil

100 g/4 oz seedless raisins
100 g/4 oz pine-nuts

Wash the spinach thoroughly. (The easiest way is to put it into a large bowl of cold water, and swirl well, then pull the leaves out one by one.) Place in a large pan and add the lemon juice but no water: the washing water still on the leaves is enough. Cook until the leaves are reduced (8–10 minutes). Drain and squeeze dry.

Meanwhile heat the oil in a pan and fry the raisins and pine-nuts until the nuts are golden.

Add the spinach, season with salt and pepper and cook for a further 2 minutes, turning the spinach all the time.

Serve hot; or cold with vinaigrette as a salad.

Ensalada de tomates   Tomato salad

As is so often the case, the simplest food is the best. This straight-forward salad is no exception. For 4 people.

6 firm, red, medium tomatoes	*wineglassful of vinaigrette (page*
salt	*204)*

Pour boiling water over the tomatoes and leave for a minute or two. Remove the skins – they should come away easily. Slice tomatoes quite thinly and arrange on a dish. Pour vinaigrette and salt over them. A good idea is to refrigerate them for 1 hour before serving.

Rape (*pronounced 'rapay'*)   Angler fish

The tail flesh of this hideous fish closely resembles lobster and can be treated as such, to great effect (not least moneywise!). 2 kg/4½ lb serves 4 people.

Cut off head of the angler fish, gut and skin. The fishmonger will do this for you if asked. Cut into thick uniform steaks and salt. Bake in a moderate oven for about 20 minutes. Allow to cool. Serve with a green salad and mayonnaise (page 203).

Boquerones   Anchovies and parsley butter

Nothing should interfere with the unique taste of fresh anchovies (which is quite unlike the tinned varieties) except perhaps a mild parsley butter. This quantity serves 4.

1 kg/2¼ lb fresh anchovies	parsley butter
a little flour	*110 g/4 oz butter*
8 tablespoons olive oil	*3 tablespoons parsley, chopped very*
1 lemon	*fine*

Wash the anchovies and shake dry. Sprinkle with salt, then roll in flour.

Heat olive oil in pan until very hot – a haze will rise when it is the correct temperature. Fry anchovies until crisp.

To make the parsley butter; warm a bowl with hot water; mash the butter in it with very finely chopped parsley. Keep cool or, better, refrigerate.

Serve anchovies with parsley butter and a quarter of lemon.

Anchovies are equally good grilled.

Moraga de sardinas a la Grenadina Sardines in the Granada style

This is a useful variation if you tire of the eternal grilled sardine. Serves 4.

1¹/₂ tablespoons olive oil	2 wineglasses white wine or 1 of
3 cloves garlic, crushed	wine and 1 of sherry
1 kg/2¹/₄ lb fresh sardines	1 tablespoon chopped parsley
juice of a lemon	

Heat the oil and add the garlic. When garlic has cooked to a light brown colour add sardines, lemon juice, wine and parsley. Just bring to boiling point. Cover and simmer for 15 minutes.

Serve with potatoes.

Besugo al horno Baked bream

A traditional way of cooking a popular Spanish fish. All of the many species of bream can be treated this way, as well as other oily fish like mackerel. Serves 4.

1 large bream (around 1 kg/2¹/₄ lb)	4 tablespoons olive oil
1 lemon	1 wineglass dry sherry (white wine
2 potatoes	will do)

Clean the fish. Make two slanting incisions in each side. Insert a slice of lemon in each cut.

Peel the potatoes and cut into thick slices. Heat the oil in a pan and fry potatoes until crisp. Lay out potatoes evenly in an oven dish. Lay fish on top. Sprinkle with salt and pepper and squeeze over the juice from the remainder of lemon. Add the sherry or white wine.

Bake in a moderate oven for about 40 minutes.

Serve with a green or tomato salad.

Trucha al horno   Baked trout

The artificial breeding of trout has slightly impaired their exquisite flavour but greatly reduced their price. This is a traditional Basque recipe that combines simplicity of preparation and a tasty result. Serves 4.

4 trout, cleaned and gutted
2 tablespoons olive oil
2 tablespoons parsley, finely chopped

juice of a lemon
30 g/1 oz butter

Wash the fish in cold water and wipe dry.

Mix the oil, half the parsley, salt, pepper and half the lemon juice and pour over the fish. Make sure they are all covered with the mixture. Leave for at least an hour to marinate.

Preheat the oven to moderate. Bake the trout for 20 minutes.

When nearly ready melt the butter in a pan, add the remaining parsley and lemon juice. Serve the trout with the hot butter; or allow fish to cool and serve cold.

Angulas   Baby eels

A great delicacy in Spain, baby eels are traditionally eaten with wooden forks which are given away in restaurants as mementos.

Baby eels are deep fried in smoking–hot olive oil and are cooked in an instant.

Serve immediately.

Lamprea   Lamprey

I am including this recipe for *lamprea* as it can equally well be used for all the different kinds of eel found in the Mediterranean and Atlantic. They are dangerous and ugly brutes (as King John would have testified had he lived), but worth the trouble of cooking them. This recipe sounds alarming but tastes fine.

1 lamprey (or lampreys) of around
*   1 kg/2¹/₄ lb*
the livers of the fish
2 onions, whole

3 wineglasses white wine
8 tablespoons olive oil
the blood of the fish

Remove the two poison sacs on the back of the lamprey if the fishmonger has not already done so. Wash in several changes of water. Remove the heads and clean, making sure you catch the blood. Remove the livers.

Put the lampreys, livers, whole onions, wine and oil in a heavy pan with a lid. Bring to the boil and simmer for 2 hours.

Remove the onions and livers. Mash them together and mix with the blood. Return them to the pan to thicken the sauce.

Serve with rice.

Raya a la Malaguena   Skate cooked in the style of Malaga

A slightly fiddly recipe but the richness of the skate makes it well worth the effort. Serves 4.

large piece(s) skate, around
  1 kg/2¹/₄ lb in all
4 tablespoons olive oil
1 slice bread, crumbled
10 almonds, blanched and peeled
parsley, chopped

3 large onions, sliced thinly
1 clove garlic
3 medium tomatoes, peeled,
  de-seeded and chopped
a pinch of saffron

Cut the skate into 4 pieces and place in an oven-proof dish. Salt lightly. Heat oven to moderate.

Heat the olive oil in pan and fry the bread, almonds and parsley until they are all light brown. Remove from pan. Crush all these ingredients together.

In the same oil fry the onions and garlic until soft brown. Add the tomatoes (minus the seeds) and the saffron.

Put the fish in the oven, which should be properly hot by now. Cook the mixture for 10 minutes, slowly. If runny pour off some of the liquid, then add to the almond mixture. Pour all the sauce over the fish. Sprinkle with salt and pepper and cook in the oven for another 10–15 minutes.

Serve with rice.

Merluza al horno   Baked hake

There is much to commend the hake as a fish: its delicate flavour, constant availability and cheapness. So I drink a toast to the hake and offer this recipe to you! Serves 4.

1 medium hake (around 1 kg/2¹/₄ lb) – or other whole fish	*50 g/2 oz butter*
	2 shallots or 1 onion
	parsley, finely chopped
2 cloves garlic, chopped	*1 wineglass sherry (dry white wine*
slice of bread, crumbled	*will do)*

Wash and dry the prepared hake. Set oven to moderate. Mix the chopped garlic, half the butter, the breadcrumbs and a little salt and pepper in a bowl. Butter an oven-proof dish with the remaining butter. Cover the fish with the mixture and lay it in the dish along with the peeled shallots (or peeled and quartered onions).

Bake in the oven for 20 minutes. Sprinkle the parsley over the fish and add the sherry. Cook for a further 10 minutes and serve with rice.

Mujol a la sal   Grey mullet baked in rock salt

This is an interesting way of cooking fish, but its real value rests on the price and availability of rock salt. Any largish fish can be done this way, the cooking time depending on its size. Serves 4.

1 grey mullet or similar fish, around 1 kg/2¹/₄ lb	*rock salt or coarse sea salt in quantity*

Wash the fish. Gut it very neatly, but leave head, tail and scales on.

Choose a deep oven-proof dish and cover the bottom with a good layer of rock salt. Place the fish firmly into this bed and cover the whole fish completely with more salt. Firm the salt down and put in a medium oven. Bake for an hour.

When you remove it, you will find the fish has been cocooned by the salt. Break it with a hefty tap and peel salt pieces off. It will bring the skin with it, leaving the succulent flesh behind.

Fritura mixta de pescados pequeños   Mixed fried fish

An excellent dish to be found on every Spanish menu – and very easy to emulate in the kitchen. The shopping for this dish is simple – merely ask the fishmonger for a bag of mixed small fish (see page 64). Serves 4.

1 kg/2¹/₄ lb mixed fish – should   *flour*
    include sardines, anchovies, tiny   *300 ml/¹/₂ pt olive oil*
    squid, red mullet, and a small   *1 lemon, quartered*
    flat fish

Clean the fish, wash in cold water and shake dry. Roll in flour.
    Heat the olive oil until it begins to smoke, then drop the fish in and fry quickly until crisp. Serve piping hot with a green salad.

Calamares a la Romana   Squid in batter

An admirable way of preparing a cheap, plentiful 'fish', and one that is much maligned because of its slimy appearance. You can cook all tender white fish, such as hake slices, in this manner. Serves 4.

6 medium squid   *300 ml/¹/₂ pt olive oil*
a little flour   *2 eggs, beaten*

Wash the squid thoroughly and then dry. Cut the body into thin rings, no more than 1 cm/½ in. wide. Cut the tentacles into short sections. Roll in flour.
    Heat the olive oil in a pan until it smokes. Dunk the floured pieces of squid into the beaten egg, then immerse in the hot oil. They will be cooked when they turn golden on all sides (within 5 minutes). Do not overcook as this makes the squid tough.

Gambas fritas   Prawns fried in their shells

There can be little to beat fresh prawns cooked on a barbecue – except perhaps fresh prawns fried in their shells! Serves 4.

4 tablespoons olive oil   *1 kg/2¹/₄ lb prawns in their shells*
2 cloves garlic, crushed   *1 tablespoon parsley, chopped*

Heat the oil in a pan and add the crushed garlic. Reduce heat. Throw in all the prawns, shaking the pan so that the oil covers them all. They will be done in about 5 minutes – then sprinkle with the chopped parsley and serve from the pan.

A common *tapas* (snack) served with drinks in Spanish bars.

Coquinas a la marinera Cockles in white wine

I have chosen this recipe as the best for preparing any of the many members of the 'bivalve' family. Serves 4.

8 tablespoons olive oil
1 medium onion, chopped
2 medium tomatoes, chopped

6 dozen small cockles (purged as
 the instruction on pages 13–14)
1 wineglass white wine
1 tablespoon parsley, chopped

Heat the olive oil in a heavy pan and fry onion gently until soft brown. Add tomatoes and cook until they are reduced to a thick sauce. Season with salt and pepper, then add white wine. Add cockles and simmer until all of them have opened. Discard any that refuse to open.

Stir in the freshly chopped parsley and serve on soup plates with fresh bread.

Zarzuela de pescado Seafood stew

Every country has its own seafood speciality, and Spain can boast one of the finest. Here it is in the simplified form. These quantities serve 4 to 6.

2 litres/3¹/₂ pints mussels (you can
 include other small shellfish, such
 as clams)
500 g/1 lb squid
angler fish, around 500 g/1 lb
4 tablespoons olive oil
1 large onion, chopped

2 cloves garlic, chopped
1¹/₂ kg/3¹/₄ lb tomatoes, skinned,
 de-seeded and chopped
1 tablespoon parsley, chopped
8 large prawns, around
 ¹/₂ litre/1 pint
1 tablespoon brandy

Clean the mussels, discarding any that are broken or do not close when tapped. Place them in a pan and heat until they open. Discard any that do not open. Remove from the pan and fork the mussels out of the shells. Clean and slice the squids into pieces not more than 1 cm/½ in. wide. Cut angler fish into squares of about 2½ cm/1 in.

Heat the oil in pan. Fry the squid until golden brown and remove. In the same oil fry the angler fish until light brown, then remove. In the same oil gently fry the onions and garlic. When they are brown add the tomatoes and parsley. Cook until reduced to a thick mush, stirring occasionally. Add mussels, squid, angler fish and prawns. Sprinkle with salt and pepper and stir in brandy.

Cover with well-fitting lid and simmer for 20 minutes.

Serve in soup bowls with plenty of fresh bread.

Paella

Paella – the national dish from the east coast of Spain which, despite the multifarious ingredients, is not difficult to make. You will need a *paellera* – a special dished iron pan with two handles. There are many recipes for *paella*; this one is fairly inexpensive and a good balance between fish and meat. It is plenty for 6 and a little extra rice will stretch it further.

6 tablespoons olive oil	12 mussels
1–1¹/₂ kg/2¹/₄–3¹/₄ lb chicken (either a small whole chicken plus some chicken pieces or all chicken pieces)	12 prawns
	4 cloves garlic
	a pinch of saffron
	4 cups rice
1 onion, finely chopped	3 tomatoes, chopped
a little flour	¹/₂ kg/1 lb cooked peas
1 kg/2¹/₄ lb fillet or leg of pork cut into large cubes	small can of red peppers (pimientos) for decoration
¹/₂ kg/1 lb hake or similar white fish	12 black and green olives, stoned

Heat half the olive oil in a pan. Roll the jointed chicken in the flour. Cook with the onion until both are golden. Remove. Seal the pork cubes in the same heated oil and remove. Again in the same oil, fry the floured hake until golden and remove.

Prepare the mussels (pages 13–14), cover with water and boil, not too fiercely, for 5 minutes until they have opened. Remove, discarding any that remain shut. Boil prawns in same liquid for 5 minutes. Remove. Strain the liquid through a tea towel or very fine sieve to remove sand and grit.

Heat the remaining olive oil in the *paellera*. Throw in three peeled cloves of garlic and remove them once they start to turn brown.

Crush a pinch of saffron with the remaining clove of garlic. Add the rice to the hot oil and fry until the rice begins to change colour (about 5 minutes). Add the garlic and saffron. Add 8 cups of the mussel/prawn water and stir as mixture comes to the boil, then simmer for 5 minutes. Stir in the chicken, pork and tomatoes and continue simmering for a further 10 minutes, shaking the dish occasionally. Add the fish, peas, prawns and then decorate with the *pimientos*, olives, mussels and shells. Simmer for a final 5 minutes.

Remove from the heat, then cover with a cloth for 7 minutes before serving in the *paellera*.

Pollo a la vasca   Basque chicken

A simple colourful recipe that makes use of those inexpensive chicken pieces so common all over Spain. The recipe also works well with veal. Serves 4.

3 tablespoons olive oil
4 chicken pieces of your choice (legs are best)
3 small red peppers (pimientos) – *canned will do*

2 onions, sliced thinly
2 tomatoes, sliced
a little flour, seasoned with salt and pepper

Heat the olive oil in a pan. Roll the chicken pieces in the flour and fry until brown on all sides. Remove from the pan.

Cut up the *pimientos*, and add them with the onions and sliced tomatoes to the hot oil. Season with salt and pepper. Cook slowly until they are all soft.

Return chicken pieces to the pan and cover. Simmer for about 1 hour.

Serve with a green or tomato salad.

Riñones al jerez   Kidneys in sherry

A fine recipe combining sherry, *salsa de tomate* and kidneys, in a typically Spanish dish. If it is very hot it can be difficult to buy kidneys. Serves 4.

1 kg/2¼ lb lambs' kidneys
a little vinegar
a little flour
30 g/1 oz butter or magarine

¼ litre/under ½ pint salsa de tomate *(page 154)*
3 glasses dry sherry
1 clove garlic, crushed

Soak the kidneys in cold water and vinegar for at least an hour. Remove the skin under a running tap, cutting away the white gristle attached to the kidney. Dry. Slice thinly with a sharp knife and dredge in salted flour.

Melt the butter in a pan and fry the kidneys for a few minutes.

Put the *salsa de tomate* in the bottom of a *cazuela* or oven-proof dish, add the kidneys, sherry and garlic and stew in a very moderate oven for 1 hour.

Serve with fresh white bread to take up the sauce.

Higado de ternera salteado con vino o jerez   Veal liver sautéed in white wine or sherry

Another excellent use of that excellent *salsa de tomate*. Serves 4.

60 g/2 oz butter
2 medium onions, chopped
1 kg/2¹⁄₄ lb calves' or lambs' liver –
ask the butcher to cut it into very
thin slices

2 tablespoons salsa de tomate
(page 154)
1 wineglass dry sherry or dry white
wine
2 tablespoons parsley, chopped

Heat the butter in a pan and cook the onions until they begin to colour. Add the liver and cook fast, turning once.

Mix the *salsa de tomate*, sherry and parsley, and season with salt and pepper. Pour over liver, sauté for 5 minutes.

Spoon sauce over the liver and serve immediately with freshly boiled potatoes.

Estofado de cordero   Spanish lamb stew

A quick recipe for dealing with the cheaper cuts of lamb; you can use the same method for pork.

1 kg/2¹⁄₄ lb best end of neck of lamb
a little flour
2 tablespoons olive oil
1 large onion, thinly sliced

2 wineglasses sherry or dry white
wine
wild marjoram or thyme

Cut up the lamb into 5 cm/2 in. cubes. Season the flour with salt and pepper and roll the meat in it so it is well covered.

Heat the oil in a pan and fry the meat quickly (4–5 minutes), turning all the time. Remove to an oven-proof dish or *cazuela*. Keep the pan hot and fry the onions until soft brown.

Cover the meat with onions, add sherry or white wine and herbs, a sprinkle of salt and a grind of pepper. Add about 3 wineglasses of water.

Stew in a slow oven for about an hour until tender.

Serve piping hot from the *cazuela* with potatoes.

Huesillos

These orange–lemon-flavoured 'fingers' have no equivalent outside Spain.

200 g/7 oz flour
100 g/3¹/₂ oz sugar
grated peel of 1 lemon
grated peel of 1 orange

6 tablespoons olive oil for the
mixture
6 tablespoons milk
4 tablespoons olive oil for frying

Sieve the flour and sugar together into a mixing bowl. Make a 'well' in the middle. Add the grated peel. Pour in the milk and oil and stir 'taking up' the flour gently.

When in a smooth dough divide up into about 10 small balls (approximately 5 cm/2 in. diameter), then elongate into 'fingers'. Cut a criss-cross on top.

Heat olive oil in a pan and fry 'fingers' until golden.

Melon con frutas   Melon surprise

There are dozens of recipes for exotic desserts but none really compares with the most natural – fresh fruit.

1 melon (any kind except a
watermelon)
a selection of fruit (peaches, pears,
plums, medlars or grapes)

1 small glass Cointreau
1 tablespoon sugar

Cut a wedge (about a third of a whole fruit) out of the melon. Scoop out the pips, then carefully scoop out the flesh.

Peel the peaches and pears and chop into a bowl with the melon flesh. Peel and pip the grapes, de-stone the plums and medlars. Mix fruit, sugar and Cointreau together and return to the hollowed-out melon. Refrigerate.

Serve cold, not forgetting the top wedge.

Sangría   Red wine punch

A part of Spain, *sangría* is drunk as an *aperitif* before the meal, during and long after! There are many recipes that include fruit, hard liquor and spices, but again the best is the simple traditional recipe.

1 bottle cheap red wine   *chopped fresh fruit – apples,*
¹/₂ bottle fizzy lemonade   *oranges, lemons, bananas*

Mix all the ingredients together in a jug and chill.

a stronger version
1 bottle dry red wine   *1 tablespoon sugar (to taste)*
1 glass Spanish brandy   *¹/₂ bottle mineral water or lemonade*
¹/₂ glass Cointreau (Curaçao will do)   *chopped fresh fruit*

Mix the day before drinking and serve chilled.

Portugal

SHOPPING

To find the true flavour of Portugal turn your back on the supermarket trolley and rows of shelves with expensive imported goods and seek out the market. There you are amply rewarded not only by the cheapness and freshness of the produce but by the atmosphere and colour of the scene. In larger towns the market trades every day except Sundays and public holidays and lasts from around 7 o'clock in the morning until about 1 o'clock in the afternoon. You find all the stalls overflowing with fresh vegetables and fruit, baskets of flowers, fresh herbs, eggs, cheeses, all flanked by sombre butchers and the *charcuterias* around the edge. You sometimes find the fishmonger in a separate building, away from the main market. Smaller towns and villages have their own travelling markets once a week.

Everything is just that little bit different, that little bit more exotic. The Portuguese cabbage is larger and a darker green, the sprouting turnip tops a novelty. Then there are the mounds of purple potato tubers (sweet potatoes) – a hangover from Portugal's colonial days. Pineapples from the 'gem of the Atlantic', the Azores, lie alongside medlars or loquats, outsize melons and lush purple figs.

Despite Portugal's long coastline and a great fishing tradition, fish is generally expensive with the exception of the fine sardine and the tasty clam.

My enthusiasm for the market must not overshadow the natural charm of the shops – the dark *mercearias* selling practically everything: wines, spirits, dairy produce, *charcuterie* and very occasionally salt cod – the former national dish of Portugal. They are open from 9 o'clock in the morning until 7 or 8 o'clock at night, closing for lunch between 1 and 3 o'clock. Half days are on Saturdays and sometimes Mondays as well. However, Monday is never a good day to shop, even in the market. The traditional Portuguese pastry shop *pastelaria*, is always busy every lunch-time and again at 4 o'clock for afternoon tea, a custom still observed here even though long since abandoned by its founders, the British. The pastry shop is open all day and every day, except Sunday, from 9 in the morning until 9 o'clock at night, sometimes later in larger towns.

The butcher *talho*, the fishmonger *peixaria*, and the baker *padaria*, open early in the morning and call it a day at lunch-time. They are open every day except Sunday, but butchers take Monday off as well. Supermarkets stay open all day, starting around 9 in the morning and closing at 9 at night.

Portuguese is a difficult language to pick up but here are a few phrases to help you get by:

Good morning	**Bom dia**
Good afternoon	**Boa tarde**
Please	**Por favor**
Thank you	**Obrigado** (masculine)
	Obrigada (feminine)
Please can I have . . . kilos of . . .?	**Dê-me por favor . . . quilos de . . . .**
That's too expensive	**Isso é muito caro**
Give me a little more, please	**Dê-me um pouco mais, por favor**
Give me a little less, please	**Dê-me um pouco menos, por favor**
Please will you cut it for me?	**Pode cortar para sopa, por favor?**
Please will you clean it for me?	**Pode prepara-lo, por favor?**

1	**um**
2	**dois**
3	**trés**
4	**quatro**
5	**cinco**
6	**seis**
7	**sete**
8	**oito**
9	**nove**
10	**dez**
100	**cem**
1000	**mil**
half	**meio/meia**
quarter	**quarto/quarta**

The Fishmonger   **A Piexaria**

Portugal, with a long Atlantic coastline, is renowned for the abundance, variety and freshness of its fish and shellfish. As no town is more than 140 miles from the coast, fresh fish is always available inland. Fish is sold in every market and sometimes from the beach when the boats come in the early morning (and perhaps in the evening as well).

Everything is sold by the kilo, except oysters which are sold by the dozen and small shellfish – like shrimps – which are sold by the 100 grams.

anchovies	**anchovas** small silver blue–green-backed fish either fresh, salted or tinned (from the grocer)
barnacles	**perceves** sold for an aperitif: surprisingly delicious
bass, rock	**cherne** wide fish with a coarse grey skin and large scales. Usually sold in steaks

bass, sea	**robalo** silver grey–blue back with white belly
bream, sea	**pargo** flat silvery pink fish with large mournful eyes. Popular and common
clams	**amêijoas** either smooth, red or grey shells, usually in good supply and fairly inexpensive
cockles	**berbigão** also called **amêijoas**
cod, salt	**bacalhau** dried and salted cod: once the national dish of Portugal but now in short supply
crab	**caranguejo**
crab, spider	**santola**
crayfish	**lavagante** similar to lobster but larger; without claws but with long antennae
cuttlefish	**chocos** like a squid but smaller and whiter
Dublin Bay prawns	**carabineiros** like tiny lobsters but with smaller pincers on fat arms
eels	**eirós, enguia**
eels, conger	**safio** sold in cutlets
gurnard	**ruivo** rose pink in colour, big bony head, tapering body
hake	**pescada** a favourite Portuguese fish: grey in colour, thin, round: sold whole, in fillets or cutlets
	pescadinha smaller hake up to 30 cm/12 in.
herring	**arenque** normally fresh but also sold either smoked or salted
lamprey	**lampreia** large ugly eel-like fish found mostly in the north. Dirty green–brown with black blotches on its skin
mackerel	**carapau** similar to British variety in appearance. Choose those with shiny skins and stiff flesh (also called **sardas**)
mackerel, horse	**cavala** has red flesh and is not as good as the other mackerel. Has dots rather than stripes
mullet, grey	**taínha** grey scales with distinctive dark line down side and white belly; common

mullet, red	**salmonete** most red fish look a bit like red mullet, but only those with two barbules hanging from their chins are the true variety
mussels	**mexilhão** now mostly cultivated on wattle fences
octopus	**polvo**
oysters	**ostras** when they can be found oysters are sold by the dozen, but most go as seedlings to France for fattening
plaice	**solha** grey flatfish with orange spots
pout	**faneca** coppery bronze with darker vertical bands and distinctive barbule on lower jaw. Common and good eating
prawns	**gambas** expensive, sold by 100 grams
sardines	**sardinhas** sardines are synonymous with Portugal. These blue–silver-backed fishes are sold everywhere; from the beach, in the market and shops and they are cooked on open fires by the roadside. Cheap, wholesome and plentiful
scabbard fish	**peixe espada** long flat brilliant silver fish sold in diagonal fillets. Very common
scorpion fish	**rascasso** rare, but a fine ingredient for fish soup. An ugly fish with spiny head, spikes and black marks on a grey skin
shad	**sável** like a very large herring, this fish is much esteemed in Portugal
shrimps	**camarões mouros** sold either cooked or uncooked

skate	**raia** only the 'wings' sold, in steaks
sole	**linguado** not strictly a sole but similar in appearance and taste. Expensive
squid	**lulas** elongated body, with long tentacles, white in colour
swordfish	**espadarte** an impressive steel blue–silvery fish with a long sharp 'beak'. Sold in slices, cutlets or steaks
trout	**truta** now all cultivated in tanks, occasionally sold alive. Not as expensive as in England
tunny	**atum** blue-backed silvery spindle-shaped fish. Often large; normally sold as steaks. Little waste and good value

The Butcher   **O Talho**

Every reasonably sized village and certainly every town has a butcher's shop and a stall or two in the covered or local market. Often they sell all those pork products *charcuterie*, as well as poultry, game and offal. Behind the butcher's counter should be (but rarely is!) a poster showing all the cuts of meat.

Beef   **Bifes**
Beef in Portugal can be tough as the meat sold as beef is sometimes cow, *vaca*.

brisket	**maca do peito com osso**
chuck end – roughly	**maca do peito**
fillet steak or chateaubriand	**filé or lombo**
flank	**peito**
neck	**cachaço**
ribs	**entrecosto**
rump steak	**alcatra**
shin of beef	**mão**
shoulder	**pá**
sirloin	**rosbife** or **vasia**
topside	**pojadouro**

Veal **Vitela**

Although expensive, veal is a good buy as it is usually tender, coming from a young beef animal killed before it has fully grown.

best end of neck	**cachaço**
breast	**peito**
chump end of loin	**rosbife**
escalope	**bife ou escalope**
knuckle	**chambão**
rump steak	**alcatra**
shoulder	**pá**

Goat **Cabrito**

Goat is sold all over Portugal. It is either sold whole for roasting – too large for the average family on holiday! – or butchered like lamb. It is good eating as long as it is *cabrito*, a kid.

Lamb **Borrego**

Lamb is comparatively cheap and can be relied on to be good. Mutton *carneiro*, fortunately is rare as they are kept for breeding and wool.

breast of lamb	**peito**
chops – including the rack	**vão de costeletas**
leg	**perna**
loin	**lombo**
loin chops	**costeletas**
saddle	**sela** a cut across the back making a double chop or roast
shoulder	**pá** a good buy boned for roasting (*pá enrolada*)

Pork **Porco**

Pork is always a good buy in Portugal and comparatively inexpensive. There is sometimes a separate stall in the market that only sells pork but more often it is sold with the rest of the meat in the *talho*.

belly	**peito**
chops	**costeletas** collective name for all chops along the back
hand	**entremeada**

knuckle	**chispe** the lower part of the leg
leg	**perna** the upper part of the leg
loin	**lombo**
loin chops	**costeleta lombo**
shoulder	**cachaço**
trotters	**pe de porco**

Offal **Ferssura**

Offal is eaten a great deal in Portugal, particularly liver in Lisbon and tripe in Oporto.

brains	**miolos**
calves' foot	**mão de vitela**
kidneys	**rins**
liver	**figado**
tongue, fresh	**língua**
tripe	**dobrada**

Game and Poultry **Aves Domésticas e Caça**

chicken	**frango** sold either whole or in pieces
boiling fowl	**galinha** common and relatively inexpensive
duck	**pato** also sold in markets, quite common
goose	**ganso** common fare in Portugal
guinea fowl	**galinha do campo** not uncommon and not too expensive
hare	**lebre** common fare
partridge	**perdiz** sold individually, plentiful and inexpensive
pigeon	**pombo** plentiful and cheap – buy dressed
quail	**codorniz** very common all the year round and quite inexpensive
rabbit	**coelho** sold everywhere and cheap
turkey	**perú** sold whole, or more commonly in pieces or squares ready for stews

The Delicatessen **A Charcutaria**

The *charcutaria* sells everything to do with the pig except fresh pork, together with cheeses, pâtés and ready-prepared dishes. There are many different sausages and cheeses, which are peculiar to each region and too numerous to list (all cheeses have the name of the village or region where they are made). However those on sale generally include:

Charcuterie	**Enchidos**
bacon	**toucinho** or **entremeado** the nearest equivalent to British bacon, from the fat belly of the pig
ham	**presunto** fine leg of pork, salted and dried for at least 6 months
ham, York	**fiambre** rolled boned ham
pork fat	**banha** sold by the kilo and widely used in Portuguese recipes. Also sold by the butcher
sausages, blood	**morcela** or **mouros** similar to black pudding
sausages, dried	**farinheiras** smoked, spiced, minced pork with rye flour
	chouriços, paio chunks of pork loin
	linguiça minced pork
	paizinho solid loin of pork smoked
sausages, fresh	**salsichas**
sucking pig	**leitão** roast baby pig, common and sold either whole by the kilo or even in slices for sandwiches

Cheese	**Queijo**
ewes' milk cheese	**queijo do Alentejo** hard cheese matured for at least 2 years
	queijo de Azeitão small individual cream cheeses
	queijo da Serra semi-hard cheese, creamy consistency with a distinctive flavour
goats' milk cheese	**queijo de Évora** hard cheese for grating
	queijo de ovelha soft creamy cheese
	requeijão a crumbly cheese
cows' milk cheese	**queijo castelão** identical to Dutch Edam
	queijo flamengo

Dairy   **Laticínios**
Very occasionally there are separate dairies in Portugal, but more
often milk and dairy products are bought in the *mercearia*

butter	**manteiga** unsalted, medium salted and salted are available, all sold packaged
cream	**natas** sold in foil packets
eggs	**ovos** sold either by the dozen or half-dozen or even singly; four qualities by grades A–D (D the best)
milk	**leite**

The General Store   **A Mercearia**

Another example of a shop which sells a wide variety of fresh and
dry goods (like our delicatessen), among them fruits, vegetables,
wines and spirits, bread and dairy produce.

capers	**alcaparras** sold either fresh or dry
chilli	**malagueta** small red peppers for *piri piri* – hot Portuguese sauce
chocolate	**chocolate**
cloves	**cravinho**
coffee	**café** formerly imported from Angola (and very bitter). More palatable varieties now come from South America
cumin	**cominhos** common spice, now sold packaged for curries
curry powder	**caril**
flour, maize	**farinha de milho**
flour, wheat	**farinha de trigo**
mineral water	**água mineral**
mustard	**mostarda**
oil, corn	**óleo de milho**
oil, olive	**azeite** Portuguese oil tends to be dark with a slightly salty tang
oil, peanut	**óleo de amendoim**
oil, sunflower	**óleo de girassol**
pepper	**pimenta** – black or white, powder or peppercorns
rice	**arroz** long-grained rice *agulha* is excellent, but expensive
saffron powder	**açafrão**

salt	**sal**
salt cod	**bacalhau** once the most common single ingredient in Portuguese cookery but now scarce and expensive, although still served in restaurants
sugar	**açucar;**, finer **açucar Mascarado**
tea	**chá** very popular in Portugal sold in packets, tea-bags or loose in specialist shops. Most English brands available
vinegar	**vinagre**

Pastries & Cakes

The Bakery   **A Padaria**
The Pastry Shop   **A Pastelaria**

The Portuguese must have the sweetest tooth in Europe, an addiction well catered for in the variety and sweetness of their cakes and pastries. They are sold (together with bread, wine and spirits, and sometimes cheese) to be eaten there or taken away. The almost forgotten English habit of 'taking afternoon tea' *chá* is much alive in Portugal, as demonstrated by the packed *pastelarias* in the mid afternoon.

Bread   **Pão**

There are as many different types of bread in Portugal as there are districts, including:

pão caseiro home-baked bread
pão de centeiro rye bread
pão de milho maize bread
pão de trigo wheat bread
regueifa large, crusty ring

Portugal is so well endowed with cakes, pastries and biscuits that it would be impossible to list the multifarious varieties. Here are some of the more common which can be found all over Portugal.

Biscuits   **Bolos Secos**

almond biscuits	**amendoas** almond-paste biscuits, very common
	gragoia almond biscuits with chocolate
cakes	**bolos** usually sponge cakes, filled with jam and topped with fresh cream
	bolo Inglês light sponge fruit cake with fruit and cherries
	Bolo Rei Kings Cake: a large, circular sweet bread filled with currants, cherries, almonds and figs with a lucky charm and an unlucky horse-bean
	guardanapos small triangular sponge cakes filled with jam, called 'napkins'
	pão-de-ló a Portuguese speciality

Pastries   **Pasteis**

éclair	**du chaise esquimós**
egg threads	**fios de ovos** great Portuguese delicacy of spun egg whites and sugar
Jesuits	**Jesuitas** wedge-shaped puff pastry with chocolate
meringues	**suspiros** or **dedos**
tart, apple	**tarte de maçã**
tart, cherry	**tarte de cereja**
tart, orange	**tarte de laranja**

Savouries **Salgados**

chancas small triangular pasties filled with highly spiced meat
croquetes oblong meat savories
empadinhas chicken pie
folhados sausage rolls
pasteis pasties – flaky pastry filled with salt cod, shrimp or
 meat

The Greengrocer **O Lugar da Hortalicas**

The open markets and shops are always full of a fine selection of
fresh vegetables *legumes*, fruit and flowers. The selection was even
wider when Portugal had her African colonies of Mozambique and
Angola, which produced exotic fruits. However, subtropical fruits
and vegetables do still come to Portugal, from the Azores. Most
vegetables are sold by the kilo.

Vegetables	Legumes
asparagus	**espargos** in season late spring, early summer: sold by the bundle. Wild asparagus is smaller and darker green and best used for omelettes
aubergines or egg plants	**berinjelas** sometimes small, oval and white, but more often large and purple
artichoke	**alcachofra** very common, inexpensive vegetable with tough, spiky green–purple, overlapping leaves
bay leaves	**folhas de louro** sold by the spray or given free with a large order
beans, broad	**favas** a common vegetable, sold most of the year; sometimes eaten raw with drinks
beans, french	**feijão verde**
beetroot	**beterraba**
broccoli	**brocolos**
Brussels sprouts	**couve de bruxelas**
cabbage, Portuguese	**couve Portuguesa** the vegetable of Portugal. It is larger and darker green than British varieties. Leaves are sold by the kilo sometimes shredded (with other vegetables) ready for the national soup *caldo verde*

carrots	**cenouras**
cauliflower	**couve flor** common all year round. Sold individually but charged by the kilo
celery	**aipo**
cucumber	**pepino** sold by the piece – sometimes half
garlic	**alho** sold by the head *cabeça*
leek	**alho-porro**
lettuce	**alface**
lupin seeds	**tremoços** large yellow seeds (similar to maize seeds) sold everywhere, including out of large drums on the roadside. Eaten raw in beer houses *cervejarias*
marrow	**chu-chú** sometimes seen in *courgette* (baby) size. When large they are sold by the piece, but charged by the kilo
mushrooms	**cogumelo** now only the cultivated button mushrooms sold, although they can be quite large; usually light brown
onions	**cebolas**
onions, spring	**cebolinha**
parsley	**salsa** large flat leaves sometimes with edible stalks
peas	**ervilhas**
peppers, red	**pimentos** smaller peppers used for hot sauces (*piri piri*) and frying, the larger for stuffing
peppers, green	**pimentos verdes** not so strong
potatoes	**batatas**
potatoes, sweet	**batatas doces**
pumpkin	**abóbora** if small sold whole and charged by the kilo; more often they are vast, so cut up and sold by the piece
radishes	**rabanetes** sold by the bunch
spinach	**espinafres** very common vegetables with several varieties
thyme, wild thyme	**cheiros**, **tomilho** both sold by the bunch, or given free of charge in sprigs if the order is large enough
tomatoes	**tomates** either red or green: red better for salads, green are harder and better for cooking

turnips	**nabos** sold either by the bunch or kilo
turnip tops	**grelos** looks like kale
watercress	**agriões** common all year round, sold by the bunch

Fruit   **Fruta**

apples	**maçãs** the golden varieties best for eating, **raineta** for cooking
apricots	**alperces** famous Portuguese fruit, fresh or dried
bananas	**bananas** imported in quantity from the Azores
cherries	**cerejas**
damsons	**damascos**
figs	**figos** cheap, plentiful and good, either green, purple or deep red
grapes	**uvas** the season for dessert grapes (black, red or white) is earlier than in most countries
grapefruit	**toranja** some locally grown but most imported; sold by the kilo
greengages	**ameixas rainhas** plum family, light green to yellow skins with yellow flesh
lemons	**limões** excellent, cheap and plentiful. Two varieties – yellow less sour than the green
loquats or medlars	**néspera** orange–yellow fruit with brown blotches: two or three pips in orange flesh. Cheap and plentiful in season (late spring and all summer)
melon	**melão** either ogden, small and round with succulent orange flesh, or honeydew, whose best varieties are from the Ribatejo and Tavira regions
melon, water	**melancia** dark green skin and red watery flesh, black pips; usually large and sold by the piece; very cheap
oranges	**laranjas** local, plentiful and cheap with long season. Best variety are seedless **baia**
peaches	**pêssegos** inexpensive, sold by the piece

pears	**peras** many good varieties, the best a small brown pear called **carapinheira**
pineapple	**ananas** imported from the volcanic Azores island of St Michael, and sold individually
plums	**ameixa** useful fruit with long summer season
raspberries	**framboesas** delicious but expensive
strawberries	**morangos** cheap and plentiful when in season
tangerines	**tangerinas**

Wines

Britain has had a long and close association with Portugal since the fourteenth century. Trade, and in particular the wine trade, flourished from the seventeenth century when Portuguese wines replaced claret (a heavy French wine that had become indispensable to the English) during the endless wars with France. As a result, vast areas of unproductive hillsides in the north were planted up with vines. During the eighteenth century brandy was added to the wine, as it stopped fermentation and the wines travelled better. These 'fortified wines' are the modern port and madeira.

Port
Practically all port is exported, formerly to England but now the French also drink it extensively:

Vintage port very expensive and not that common in Portugal
Tawny port a much lighter and paler port
Late bottle vintage a blend of wines grown in the same year.
   Again lighter than the vintage port but still good drinking

White port a comparatively new drink and excellent as an aperitif. Serve chilled

The brand names are mostly English or Scottish as the original *quintas* (estate) owners were all British – Croft, Sandeman, Taylor, Graham.

Madeira

An excellent wine served as an aperitif when dry *sercial* or medium-dry *verdelho*. The heavier, fruitier Madeiras, such as sweet *Bual* and medium-dry *Malmsey* (which was the undoing of the Duke of Clarence) are better drunk with the dessert or, as quite common in Portugal, with cheese.

Vinhos verdes

Produced between the Douro and Minho from vines grown high up in the trees and on trellises, the wine is delicate and crisp and very refreshing for the summer. The word *verde* refers to the youthfulness of the wine and not to the colour (which is either a pale yellow or red). Red vinho is widely drunk in Portugal, but may be a little sharp for British taste. Brand names include *Gatão*, *Lagosta*, *Ribeiros*, *Alvarinho*, *Acácio*, *Vilacetinho*, *Quinta da Aveleda*.

Dão

Grown in the north in the region of the river Dão, this fine red wine is matured in oak casks. It is robust and dry with a deep, almost brown colour. The FVD (Federação do Vinicultores do Dão) on the paper seal on the cork is the guarantee of an excellent wine. The younger Dãos are less heavy and good served slightly chilled. White Dão is dry, 'clean' and refreshing, particularly when served chilled.

Rosé

Forty-four million bottles of Portuguese rosé were exported in 1978 – a fair accolade for this pink sparkling wine. The best-known brand name is *Mateus*, with its distinctive round flagon, although there are plenty of others. Served chilled, these rosés are fine lunch wines.

Table wines

alcobaça (vinhos de mesa) strong, ruby-red wines with a good
    bouquet, white wines are dry, aromatic and amber in colour
alentejo red and white wines from the south. Mild and pleasant
Algarve this region produces strong, rather smooth red and white
    wines and rosé – also a good matured wine similar to sherry
bucelas a light dry fresh wine
'champagne' known as *espumantes naturais* – a sparkling wine
    made like champagne, sweet, medium or dry *brut*, or very dry
    brut de brut
colares from an area close to Lisbon and the sea, these vines have
    much to contend with – salt winds, fog and humid summers.
    Despite this they produce palatable red and white wines
pinhel a northern region producing similar wines to Dão
torres vedras an intensive wine-growing area

COOKING

Apart from the luxurious beaches in the south, Portugal is a hard
country. On two sides is the bountiful but often unfriendly Atlantic
ocean; the interior is wild, with rugged mountains and arid plains
and the climate is one of extremes. The Portuguese have evolved a
cuisine to combat these excesses, a robust cuisine; one for workers
and not for soft Latins who laze around the Mediterranean. It is
strong, virile, peasant food which has evolved over the years and
has been greatly influenced by invaders (500 years of Moorish rule
in the south), by exploration (the epic voyages of Henry the
Navigator who introduced exotic spices from Africa, South
America and the East Indies) and, to some extent, by Spanish
customs which occasionally crept over the border.

   Like her Mediterranean counterpart Spain, the basis of Portugal's cooking is olive oil, although in some northern areas pork
fat is preferred. Also in common with her neighbours, tomatoes,
onion and garlic form the basis of most sauces for both meat and
fish dishes. Fish, of course, is the staple diet of the coastal regions,
while pork and sausages are eaten in the northern mountains. Salt
cod, once the single most common dish in Portugal, is now an
expensive luxury. A pity, as there are 365 ways of cooking it! The
capital, Lisbon, and the second city, Oporto, vie with each other as
to which of their dishes is best – the liver from Lisbon or the tripe
from Oporto.

PIQUANT BARBECUE SAUCE.

2 tablespoons malt, cider or red wine vinegar
¼ pint water
2 level tablespoons sugar (demerara)
1 level tablespoon prepared mustard
½ level teaspoon pepper
1½ level teaspoons salt
¼ level teaspoon cayenne   (optional)   (or paprika)
1 thick slice lemon
1 onion, skinned and thinly sliced
2 oz butter

- - - - - - - - - - -

¼ pint tomato ketchup or 1 small tin tomato puree (2½ oz)
2 tablespoons Worcestershire sauce (opt)

Caldo verde   Cabbage soup

The soup of Portugal. It derives its name from *couve*, the large dark green cabbage. The leaves are sold finely shredded for the soup. This makes enough for 6.

4 potatoes, peeled and halved
3 tablespoons olive oil
1¹/2 litres/2¹/4 pints chicken stock
(water will do)

350 g/³/4 lb couve *(shredded cabbage)*

Boil the potatoes in the salted stock until well cooked, about twenty minutes, without covering pan. Remove and mash with the olive oil.

Add the potato and oil mixture to the stock and stir.

Add the shredded cabbage and boil uncovered for not a moment more than 3 minutes. Season with salt and pepper. Serve hot with plenty of bread.

Ovos à Portuguesa   Portuguese eggs

Simple and good for a light lunch or a starter.

for each person
1 small egg
1 large tomato
parsley, finely chopped

Cut off the tops of the tomatoes with a sharp knife. Scoop out the pulp and seeds. Stand them in a baking tray or in individual ramekin dishes. Salt the inside of the tomato cases. Break an egg into each tomato, cover with the tomato pulp (not seeds), then sprinkle with salt and pepper.

Bake in a moderate oven for about 10 minutes or until the eggs have set.

Sprinkle with parsley before serving.

Ovos mexidos com tomate   Scrambled eggs with tomatoes

Although egg dishes are not that common in Portugal, they do 'favour' the *ovos mexidos*, a rather special scrambled egg! This is a slightly more robust dish for 4.

4 tablespoons olive oil
4 slices white bread, without crusts
250 g/8 oz chouriços *(spicy*
*   sausage), sliced thinly*

250 g/8 oz butter
6 tomatoes, chopped
8 eggs
parsley, finely chopped

Heat the oil and fry the sliced bread until golden on both sides. Cover with layer of *chouriços* and keep warm on serving dish.

Melt half the butter in a pan and cook the tomatoes until soft (about 10 minutes).

Meanwhile melt half the remaining butter in a saucepan. Beat the eggs in a bowl and season with salt and pepper. Cook egg mixture over a low heat, stirring all the time with a wooden spoon.

When the eggs have jelled, but not hardened, remove from the heat and beat in the remaining butter.

Serve eggs on the toast with cooked tomatoes on top. Sprinkle with the chopped parsley.

Batatas com salsa   Potatoes in parsley sauce

The Portuguese eat a lot of potatoes, either boiled or fried, but here is a slightly more original recipe. Serves 4.

4 tablespoons olive oil
1 kg/2¹/₄ lb large potatoes, sliced
*   about 1 cm/¹/₂ in. wide*
1 onion, chopped fine

1 clove garlic, crushed
good sprig parsley, chopped fine
250 ml/8 fl. oz boiling water

Heat the olive oil in a large pan and cook the potatoes and onion until potatoes are a golden brown on both sides (about 10 minutes). Add the garlic and parsley, season with salt and pepper. Stir. Pour in the boiling water, shake over the heat occasionally but do not stir as this will break up the potato. Cover the pan and simmer gently for 10–15 minutes, until potatoes are tender. Drain off excess water.

Serve hot with meat, or cold with mayonnaise.

Favas à Portuguesa   Broad beans in the Portuguese style

Broad beans are a very common vegetable all over Portugal, with a long growing season. This recipe makes a good light lunch for 4. Don't use a tin saucepan as this will blacken the beans.

1¹/₂ kg/3 lb unshelled broad beans
  (about 750 g/1¹/₂ lb when
  shelled)
125 g/4¹/₂ oz belly of pork
  (touchino), diced
1 large onion, finely chopped

1 clove garlic, crushed
125 g/4¹/₂ oz ham (presunto), *cut*
  in strips
125 g/4¹/₂ oz smoked sausage
  (chouriços), sliced
parsley, finely chopped

Boil the broad beans in salted water for around 20 minutes.

Heat the belly of pork in a heavy pan and add onion and garlic. Cook for about 10 minutes. Season with salt and pepper.

Drain the broad beans and add to the onions and pork. Add ham, sausage and parsley. Cook slowly for a further 5 minutes.

Serve with a green and tomato salad.

Arroz com grelos a Portuguesa   Rice with turnip tops

Turnip tops are used a great deal in Portuguese cookery. Here is a substantial recipe for 4 people.

6 tablespoons olive oil
1 large onion, thinly sliced
1 large carrot, grated
500 g/1 lb rice

1 litre/1³/₄ pints chicken stock
150 g/6 oz turnip tops (the tender
  leaves only)

Heat half the olive oil and cook the onion and carrot until soft. Add the rice and cook gently for 5 minutes, shaking the pan occasionally. Add the chicken stock and cook gently until the rice has taken up all the liquid.

Meanwhile boil the turnip tops in salted water until tender (about 5 minutes). Drain well and chop.

Heat the rest of the oil in a pan. Add the chopped turnip tops and cook for 15 minutes. Add to the rice and mix well.

Serve hot or cold.

Turnip tops are also excellent boiled like spinach; or boiled, then chopped, dressed with oil and lemon juice and served as a salad.

Peixe espada grelhado   Grilled scabbard fish

Rightly a much esteemed fish dish in Portugal with all the right qualities – it's cheap, simple to make and delicious to eat! Serves 4.

4 scabbard fish steaks (these diagonally shaped steaks will be pre-prepared by the fishmonger)
juice of 1 lemon

4 tablespoons olive oil
parsley, chopped
1 lemon, quartered

Lay the steaks in a bowl and pour the lemon juice over them, making sure they are all coated with juice. Dust lightly with salt. Leave to marinate for 1 hour.

Mix oil, parsley, pepper and salt together and smear over both sides of the fish. Grill for approximately 6 minutes on each side.

Serve with a lemon quarter and a green tomato salad.

Sardinhas   Sardines

The cookery section on Portugal could not be complete without a mention of sardines, for they are found everywhere. Having mentioned them, I now refer you to page 12 for grilling instructions, and the Spanish (page 88) and Italian (page 163) sections for interesting variations which apply equally to Portugal.

Pescada cozida   Boiled hake

Hake is an excellent fish, equally good eaten hot or cold with mayonnaise. Serves 4.

1 hake around 1 kg/2¹/₄ lb, cleaned
1 onion, thinly sliced
1 carrot, thinly sliced

1 leek (if available), sliced
1 tablespoon parsley, chopped
1 bay leaf, crumbled

Put all the ingredients into a saucepan. Season with salt and pepper. Just cover with cold water and bring to the boil. Reduce heat and allow to simmer for about 15 minutes, when the fish will begin to come away from the bone. Allow to cool in the fish stock (*court-bouillon*). Remove the fish and serve with mayonnaise (page 203) or vinaigrette (page 204).

Caldeirada estilo Nazaré   Fish stew from Nazaré

Every country has a special fish stew, and every coastal district argues that theirs is the best recipe. Here is the version from Nazaré, in the Estremadura region. Serves 6.

Tell the fishmonger that you want 2 kg of fish for a *caldeirada* and he will select them for you (and fillet them, if asked). His selection should include some white fish with firm flesh, a flat fish, a squid or cuttlefish, some clams and a few mussels. If the budget goes that far, include a few prawns or even a crayfish.

8 tablespoons olive oil
3 medium onions, chopped
2 medium red peppers, seeded and
   sliced
1/2 kg/1 lb tomatoes, chopped
1 glass white wine

1 clove garlic
1 tablespoon parsley, chopped
1 bay leaf
pinch of saffron powder
2 kg/4 1/4 lb mixed fish

Heat the olive oil, add the onions and peppers and cook until the onions are a soft brown and the peppers are soft. Add the tomatoes and cook until the whole is reduced to a mush. Add the white wine, garlic, parsley, bay leaf and saffron powder and cook for a further 5 minutes, stirring occasionally.

Add the filleted white fish to the mixture and simmer for 10 minutes. If squid are used they should first be fried in the oil (before the onions). About 4 minutes will be enough, as overcooking makes them tough. It is best to transfer the whole to an oven dish to finish off in a moderate oven by cooking for a further 20 minutes. If there is no oven simmer very gently on the stove for 15 minutes.

Serve with boiled potatoes and the clams or mussels.

Caldeirada à Ribatejana   Ribatejo fish stew

Sadly today the basic ingredients of the classic fish stews, like the scorpion fish for the French *bouillabaisse*, are scarce and usually very expensive. This fish stew is good and wholesome, simple to prepare – unlike many of its counterparts – but gives the idea of using different types of fish together. This is enough for four.

4 tablespoons olive oil
1 large onion, thinly chopped
2 large tomatoes, sliced
500 ml/³⁄₄ pint water
500 g/1 lb gurnard or eel or other
    firm-fleshed fish, skinned and cut
    into chunks

500 g/1 lb hake or grey mullet or
    similar white-fleshed fish, cut
    into chunks
500 g/1 lb potatoes, diced
1 tablespoon parsley, chopped

Heat the oil in a heavy saucepan. Add the onion and garlic and cook until soft brown. Add the chopped tomatoes, water and season. Boil vigorously until the water and oil combine. Add the firm-fleshed fish and simmer for 10 minutes. Add the white-fleshed fish, potatoes and parsley and simmer for a further 15 minutes or until all the fish and potatoes are cooked. Serve with plenty of fresh bread. Do not worry if the fish disintegrates as this thickens the broth.

Bacalhau com pimentos e tomates à Setubal   Salt cod with peppers and tomatoes in the style of Setubal

Most books on Portuguese cookery begin by apologizing for including so many recipes for salt cod. I give one solely for the sake of tradition as salt cod is now difficult and expensive to buy, very troublesome to prepare and heavy on gas to cook. To those still undaunted by the task and expense I dedicate this one recipe. The result is delicious but easier to eat in a restaurant! Serves 4.

1 kg/2¹⁄₄ lb salt cod
500 g/1 lb potatoes
4 tablespoons olive oil

4 green peppers, seeded and sliced
5 tomatoes, sliced
black olives

Soak the salt cod overnight in cold water changing the water at least 4 times. Put the cod in heavy saucepan and cover with water. Bring to the boil, then simmer for 2 to 3 hours until tender. Strain and set aside.

Boil the potatoes (washed but unpeeled) in salted water until tender. Slice – not too thinly. Cover a pan with some of the oil and heat. Fry the sliced peppers until soft (about 8 to 10 minutes).

Place alternate layers of sliced potatoes, fish, peppers and tomatoes in an oven-proof dish. Sprinkle with salt and pepper. Pour the rest of the oil over the dish. Bake in a moderate oven for 20 minutes.

Serve garnished with black olives.

Galinha com arroz   Chicken with rice

A simple, economical dish – equally good hot or cold.

200 g/6 oz butter
1 dressed chicken, around
  1 kg/2¼ lbs
juice of 1 lemon

1 medium onion, sliced
300 g/11 oz rice
½ litre/1 pint chicken stock (made
  with the chicken giblets)

Melt a third of the butter in heavy casserole dish or pan. Put chicken in the dish and roll it around so it is well covered with the butter. Sprinkle with lemon juice then salt and cook in moderate oven for about 1 hour.

Meanwhile prepare the rice. Melt half remaining butter in a pan and cook the onion until a soft golden colour. Add the rice and stir, making sure all the grains are covered by the butter. Pour in the stock and dot the rice with the remaining pieces of butter. Season and cook for about 30 minutes; by then the rice should have absorbed all the liquid and be tender.

Cut the chicken into portions and serve on top of the rice, with a tomato salad.

If served cold mix a little vinaigrette with the rice.

Perdizes estufadas   Stewed partridge

Partridge is a common bird in Portugal and quite cheap. It is an excellent treat for the English, who rarely see partridges outside expensive game shops. Allow one partridge per person; these quantities are for 4.

4 partridges, plucked and dressed
2 tablespoons vinegar
3 glasses white wine
4 medium onions, thinly sliced

2 cloves garlic, crushed
3 teaspoons tomato puree
spring parsley, finely chopped

Wash and dry the partridges. Put them in a casserole or heavy saucepan with a tight-fitting lid. Pour in olive oil, vinegar and white wine, and season with salt and pepper. Stew slowly for 30 minutes with cover on.

Add onions, garlic, tomato puree and parsley, and simmer for another 30 minutes. (Add extra wine if it is too dry.)

Serve hot with a green vegetable, or cold with *molho de Vilao*, a vinaigrette made from:

6 tablespoons olive oil	*1 tablespoon chopped parsley*
3 tablespoons vinegar	*1 tablespoon capers*
1/2 chopped onion	

well mixed and seasoned.

Coelho guisado com arroz   Stewed rabbit with rice

Rabbit has always been popular on the continent and Portugal is no exception. Here is a recipe to refresh your memory as to how good rabbits are; enough for 4.

2 onions, chopped	*1 clove garlic*
2 wineglasses white wine	*150 g/5 oz spicy sausage*
1 carrot, thinly sliced	*(chouriços)*
thyme	*3 large tomatoes, chopped*
1 young rabbit	*225 g/8 oz rice*
50 g/2 oz butter	

Mix one of the onions, white wine, carrot, thyme and salt and pepper together in a large saucepan. Cut up the rabbit (or ask the butcher to do it for you) and leave to marinate for 1 hour in this mixture. Cook the rabbit over low heat or in a moderate oven in the marinade for about 1 hour, or until tender.

When the rabbit has been cooking for $\frac{1}{2}$ hour, melt the butter in a large pan and cook the second onion until soft brown. Add the crushed garlic, sausage and tomato. Season with salt and pepper.

Add about 1 litre of water to the pan. Transfer the rabbit to this pan and add the rice, stirring once. Cook together for 20 minutes.

Serve with a green salad.

Carneiro recheado   Stuffed lamb

So simple a recipe, so quick to prepare and so wonderful to eat.
What more could you ask? Enough for 4.

25 g/1 oz butter
1 large onion, chopped finely
50 g/2 oz almonds, peeled, blanched
   and chopped
a handful of breadcrumbs
grated rind of 1 lemon

20 green olives, stoned
1 egg
1 loin of lamb (boned), around
   1 kg/2¹/₄ lb
1 glass dry white wine

Melt the butter in a pan and cook the onion until a soft brown. Add
the almonds, breadcrumbs, lemon rind and olives, season with salt
and pepper. Remove from the heat.

Beat the egg and add to the pan. Mix well. Add more breadcrumbs if too runny. Spread the mixture over the meat then roll up,
tying it with a piece of string. Place in a baking dish, rub with salt
and pour the wine over.

Bake in a moderate oven until tender (about 1 hour). Baste
occasionally. Serve with potatoes and a green vegetable.

Porco com amêijoas   Pork with clams

The interesting contrast between the flavour of the pork and clams
is well worth the trouble of marinating the meat.

750 g/1¹/₂ lb lean pork
¹/₃ litre/¹/₂ pt dry white wine
4 tablespoons vinegar
1 bay leaf
2 cloves
3 cloves garlic, crushed

100 g/2 oz pork fat (or use butter or
   oil)
2 large onions, sliced
3 large tomatoes, chopped
30 clams

Cut the meat into 2½ cm/1 in. cubes. Put the wine, vinegar, bay leaf,
cloves and 2 of the cloves of garlic into a deep dish and stir. Add the
meat cubes, making sure they are all covered with the wine mixture. Cover and leave overnight to marinate.

Heat half the pork fat in a large saucepan, cook the onions until
they begin to take on colour, add the tomatoes and other clove of
garlic and cook until they are all soft.

Meanwhile prepare the clams (page 13).

Put clams into the onion–tomato mixture, having first tested to make sure they are alive (page 13), and cook fast for 5 minutes. Remove any clams that have not opened.

Heat the remaining pork fat in a large pan. Brown the pork on all sides. Add the marinade and cook slowly, uncovered, until most of the liquid has evaporated.

Serve the pork, the clams in the shells and the tomato sauce with new boiled potatoes. Garnish by sprinkling the chopped parsley over everything.

Ananas com vinho do porto   Pineapple and port

A fine mixture from Portugal and her islands, the Azores; they go together so well.

1 pineapple
sugar
2 glasses port

Peel, core and slice the pineapple. Sprinkle each slice with sugar and lay in a deep bowl. Pour the port over the pineapple and chill, turning occasionally.

Bolas de figo   Fig and almond balls

An untrue flavour – so good that I suggest double quantities!

500 g/1 lb fresh figs
400 g/14 oz almonds, blanched
75 g/3 oz cooking chocolate
300 g/10 oz sugar (preferably caster)

outer peel of an orange (not the pith)
1 wineglass water

Mince the orange peel, almonds, figs and chocolate together. (Or chop the orange peel, almonds and figs, and grate the chocolate.) Then mix with chopped figs, orange peel and crushed almonds.

Boil water and sugar for 3 minutes until it becomes syrupy. Add the fig mixture and stir in well. Turn on to a plate and allow to cool.

Roll into little balls in caster sugar.

Serve with coffee.

Italy

SHOPPING

One of the great joys of Italy is to be caught in the colours and sounds of the local food market. Amid the bustle and high-pitched chatter black-clad widows shop and gossip alongside their daughters and grand-daughters dressed in bright clothes. They bargain under a confusion of striped awnings and umbrellas, carefully selecting their food. It is a miscellany of colour and shapes, the many shades of green vegetables and salads; the vivid splashes of red tomatoes built high into pyramids; pink and silver fish dotted with yellow lemons; orange medlars and apricots; the gaping water melons with crimson flesh and black seeds, and the stalls hung with sausages, salami and cheeses.

To catch the best of the market you must go early – about 8 o'clock – as there is little left by mid-day or 1 o'clock. In the smaller towns and villages the market appears only once, or possibly twice, a week and then is combined with clothes, excellent pottery, toys, and household bits and pieces. Larger towns have permanent covered markets which are open every morning except Sunday. Villages on the coast also have permanent daily markets but only for fish, the general market being set up in another part of the village.

The shops are no less colourful in their display of fine produce. They keep longer hours than the markets, generally opening at 8 and closing for a long lunch between 1 and half past 4, then staying open until 7 or 8 at night. The shops shut for one afternoon during the week (usually the one afternoon you have set aside for shopping), and on Saturday afternoons. (Larger supermarkets may stay open all day regardless of the custom of the town.) There is no set rule for opening time and they vary from place to place. Remember – time spent in reconnaissance is never wasted!

A few simple phrases should endear you to the stall-holder so you end up with what you need and how you want it! Good luck.

Good morning	**Buon giorno**
Good evening	**Buona sera**
Please	**Per favore, per cortesia**
Thank you	**Grazie**
Please can I have . . . kilos of . . .	**Per favore mi dai ... kili di . . .**
That's too expensive	**Troppo caro**
Give me a little more, please	**Me ne dia un po'oli piu**
Give me a little less, please	**Me ne dia un po'oli meno**
Can you cut it up for me, please?	**Lo taglia in pezzi, per cortesia?**
Can you clean it for me, please?	**Lo pulisce per me, per favore?**
1	**uno/una**
2	**due**
3	**tre**
4	**quattro**
5	**cinque**
6	**sei**
7	**sette**
8	**otto**
9	**nove**
10	**dieci**
100	**cento**
1000	**mille**
half	**mezzo**
quarter	**quarto**
100 grams of . . .	**un etto di . . .**

The Fishmonger   **La Pesceria**

Three thousand years of intensive fishing and the illegal use of dynamite have taken a heavy toll on the stocks of fish *pesca* in the Mediterranean and nowhere is this more evident than in parts of Italy. There is still a steady supply of fresh fish – mostly, alas, rather small – but now much is imported frozen, then thawed and sold as fresh fish. Imagine the horror of discovering that *calamari* (squid) had been imported frozen from Japan and sold on the slab in Puerto Ercoli.

anchovy	**alici, acciughe** tiny fish with large mouth; blue–black in colour, silver sides. Caught only on a waning moon
angler fish	**pescatrice** grotesque, large broad flat head with sharp teeth and three long 'filaments'. Colour depends on its last surroundings but usually grey–white with brown marks
bass, sea	**spigola** a round silvery fish with grey–blue back and silver underside. Expensive, sometimes bred artificially or imported
bream, gilt-head	**orata** silver fish with golden spots on each cheek and a crescent between the eyes
bream, sea	**pagro** silver fish with pink fins – sometimes sold as *dentice Atlantico*
carpet shells	**vongole nere** greyish in colour, darker in the middle with concentric fine line. Common and inexpensive
cockles	**cuore edule** or **coccioli** white corrugated shell
dentex	**dentice** silver fish with steel-blue back and reddish fins. Good eating, expensive – mostly imported
dogfish	**palombo** one of the shark family. Grey with white spots on back and sides. Medium-priced, common, good white 'meat'. Sold skinned in pieces
Dublin Bay prawns	**scampi** rose grey in colour, a miniature lobster with outsize pincers. Found on Adriatic coast

garfish — **anguillia** long, thin pipe fish with needle-sharp teeth in crocodile jaws. Bright blue–green back with silver belly. Bones are turquoise! Common and inexpensive

gurnard — **gallinella** happy-looking fish! Reddish yellow, even grey, back with bright red fins. Common and cheap

hake — **merluzzo**, **nasello** an excellent fish with a long round slender body and scaly silver–grey skin. Sold in steaks, cutlets or whole

inkfish or cuttlefish — **seppie** oval creatures with eight short tentacles and two long. No set colour although sometimes zebra-striped. Secretes sepia-coloured ink (hence name). When local, inexpensive

John Dory — **pesce San Pietro**, **sampietro** this ugly, miserable-looking fish, grey to olive brown with a yellow metallic sheen, has a distinctive black spot on its back – this being the Apostle's thumb-mark when he caught it in the Sea of Galilee. Good eating

lamprey — **lampreda marina** greenish–grey or olive-brown eel with black marbling and dirty white belly. Quite common and good eating

mackerel, Atlantic — **sgombro** dark blue back with bright blue–green stripes and silver belly. Cheap and plentiful

mackerel, horse or scad — **suro** not strictly a mackerel but as good to eat. Large eyes, lozenge-shaped scales in stepped lateral line. Light greenish-blue back, silver stomach

mullet, grey — **cefalo** leaden blue–grey back with paler underparts. Quite common and inexpensive – sometimes artificially bred

mullet, red — **triglia** bright rose in colour with two distinct barbules on its chin. Names vary – **tregghia** in the south

mussels	**muscoli**, **cozze** blue–black shells. Now all those sold are cultivated
octopus	**polpo** common and not expensive; best varieties have two rows of suckers on their tentacles
oysters	**ostriche** now mostly cultivated. Avoid the larger wild varieties which can be dangerous
prawns	**gamberetti** plentiful in summer, but expensive. Sold by the *etto*
	mazzancolle larger, better eating variety
sardines	**sarde**, **sardine** very plentiful and cheap fish with greenish back and silver belly and sides. Common all year round – best May to September
scorpion fish	**scorfano** ugly brown-spotted camouflaged fish with blotchy markings. Oblong with high back, poisonous spikes on back and head
sea urchins	**ricci** small black or dark red balls with vicious spikes. Must be alive, female and eaten when moon is full!
shrimp	**gamberetto grigio** sold by the *etto*
sole	**sogliola** brown or yellow–grey back to this flat, white-fronted fish. Expensive, but excellent eating
spiny lobster	**aragosta** similar to the lobster but without any claws
squid	**calamaro** usually transparent but sometimes with a hint of brown. Eight short and two long tentacles. Several varieties; flying squid **totano** have thinner bodies, longer with wide fins at the rear. Sold whole or in pieces, quite inexpensive. Now widely imported

sturgeon	**storione** fish with long snout, blue–green back embedded in the flesh, common in the Adriatic. Adequate, inexpensive flesh, usually sold in chunks like meat
swordfish	**pesce spada** a large fish with a 'beak'; silver in colour and quite common. Sold in slices or steaks, expensive but excellent eating, with little wastage
trout	**trota** now they are artificially bred and relatively cheap
tunny	**tonno** large fish with dark blue back, silver skin and pale pink flesh. Sold in joints or steaks. Go for the belly meat **ventresca**
turbot	**rombo** flat fish, brownish yellow–grey with black and white spots. Good eating and not too expensive

The Butcher   **La Macelleria**

The Italian butcher sells all kinds of meat, poultry and game. The fertile plains of the north produce excellent beef (most notably veal, for which Italy is so famous), while the more arid south produces sheep, lambs and goats. Where all meat can be bought in the north good beef in the south is expensive (loaded with transport costs) and is much more likely to be a worked-out ox or spent cow. Veal is the exception to this. Pork may be unobtainable during the hot summer months in the south.

Beef   **Carne di bue**
The Italian cuts of beef are slightly different to the English, but not unrecognizable. Their meat is well butchered and joints are tied ready for roasting.

brisket	**petto**
fillet steak or chateaubriand	**filetto**
flank	**fianchetta**
leg	**muscolo**
neck	**collo**

ribs and part of shoulder	**braciola**
rib steak	**bistecca alla Fiorentina**
rump steak	**colarda**
shin	**muscolo**
shoulder	**spalla**
silverside	**sotto fesa**
sirloin	**controfiletto**
topside	**fesa**

Veal   **Vitello** (calf); **Vitellone** (young beef)

best end of neck	**costaletta**
breast	**petto** or **pancia**
chops	**costata**
chump end of loin	**costato**
escalope	**scalopine**
knuckle	**osso bucco**
loin	**filetto**
neck	**collo**
shoulder	**spalla**
topside	**noce**

Goat   **Capra**

Goat and kid *capretto* are not common in Italy but occasionally found in the larger cities, in the south and in Sardinia. The cuts are identical to lamb.

Lamb   **Agnello**

Traditionally lamb has been a good buy whose quality belies its price, and lamb in Italy is no exception.

best end of neck	**cotolette**
breast	**petto**
leg	**coscia**
loin chop	**cotolette**
middle or scrag end of neck	**collo**
saddle	**sella d'agnello**
shoulder	**spalla** (boned for roasting – **rombo**)

Pork   **Carne di maiale**

Italy is world-famous for her pork products such as *prosciutto*, *salame*, etc. Fresh pork is just as good, especially around Bologna in the north.

belly	**spuntatura**
chop	**bistecca di maiale, costa di maiale**
hand or shoulder	**spalla**
knuckle or lower leg	**osso di prosciutto**
leg (boned)	**prosciutto (sensa osso)**
loin	**gola**
neck	**collo**
ribs	**petto**
tenderloin	**filetto**
trotters	**piede**

Chicken   **Pollo**

Chicken is either sold whole with all its innards, head and feet, or in pieces. There can be little to compare with a maize corn-fed chicken fresh off the market stall!

chicken	**pollo**
half chicken	**mezzo pollo**
quarter chicken	**quarto pollo**
chicken breast	**petto di pollo**
chicken leg	**coscia di pollo**
chicken liver	**fegatini**

Game	**Caccia**
duck	**anitra**
guinea fowl	**gallina faraona**
hare	**lepre**
partridge	**pernici**
quail	**quaglie**
rabbit	**coniglio**
small birds	**uccelletti**
turkey	**tacchino**

Offal	**Coratella**
brains	**cervello**
kidneys	**rognoni**
liver	**fegato**
sweetbreads	**animelle**
tongue, fresh	**lingua**
tripe	**trippa**

The General Store   **La Drogheria**

Sells most dry goods and flour products.

The Delicatessen   **La Salumeria**

Sells some dry goods, mostly *charcuterie*, cheese and tins.

The Oil and Wine Shop   **Il Vino e Olio**

Sells just that.

The spread of the supermarket has forced many of the traditional specialized shops (the grocer, bakery, dairy, wine shop, etc.) to amalgamate in order to compete. As a result, most shops in Italy sell a little of everything.

Charcuterie
Everything to do with the pig once it has ceased to be fresh pork. Italy is famous for its salamis and sausages, each region priding itself that their particular recipe is superior to all others. Those products that are fairly general to all Italy are listed below:

bacon	**bacon** or **pancetta coppata** imported varieties are expensive – local bacon is merely sliced smoked belly of pork (**speck**)
ham	**prosciutto**
ham, cooked	**prosciutto cotto** similar to our York ham
ham, raw	**prosciutto crudo** Parma ham is the best known and the most expensive. **Coppa**, which is from further down the leg is as good and less expensive

mortadella	**mortadella** similar in appearance to spam. The traditional Bologna sausage made with pure pork (cheaper versions are made with all kinds of suspect meat). Pale pink in colour and up to 20 cm/9 ins. across, often with visible peppercorns. Much cheaper than all salami
salami	**salame**, plural **salami**, vary greatly in their content in the type of lean meat and in the proportion of fat as well as the method of maturing. A few of the many are:

salame Bresada good eating, lean pork speckled with pork fat

salame di Felino from the home of good pig rearing – near Parma – pure pork, little fat, local white wine, whole peppercorns and garlic. Expensive but very fine

salame Genovese pork, veal and pork fat. Very good with strong distinct flavour

salame Milano or **Crespone** most common throughout all Italy. Equal proportions of lean pork, beef and pork fat – seasoned with garlic, pepper and white wine, fine grainy appearance

salame Napoletano a spicy salami made from pork and beef with black and red pepper

The above are usually sold sliced – **affettato**

sausages	**salsicce** usually red, highly spiced and dried. Very good eating. Fresh *salsicce* sold in the butchers but not normally in the hot summer weather

salsicce di cinghiale excellent but expensive variety with wild boar and spices

Dairy products
butter

burro all sold packaged. Mostly unsalted butter. Now many foreign brands, Danish, German, etc. available

cheese

formaggio a wide and excellent variety of cheeses are produced nationally and locally. Many of the common cheeses may be either *piccante* (strong) or *dolce* (mild), and the same words are used for other foods, *salame* for instance, which come in various strengths of flavour

Bel Paese brand name for a cream cheese

cacciotta 'country cheese' from Tuscany, made from ewes' milk. Shaped like a balloon pinched near the top

dolce latte creamy blue cheese

fontina a creamy Gruyère

gorgonzola blue cheese

grana very hard cheese sold in the piece, cut with a special knife from the great 'drums' the cheese is made in, or grated. Best and most expensive is **Parmigiano** (Parmesan) from Parma; there are cheaper Italian and Argentinian varieties. It is grated and scattered on pasta dishes, but also a first-rate eating cheese

mozzarella soft white cheese (formerly made of buffalo's milk). For cooking and as a mild eating cheese. Should be bought fresh as does not keep well. Keep cool in water

peccorino hard cheese made from ewes' milk, made in small round baskets and used in same way as *grana*

provolone medium-hard

ricotta soft traditional milk cheese – unsalted (now usually cows' milk). To use straight away, eaten with sugar or with salt

sardo a ewes' milk cheese

	stracchino cream cheese
cream, fresh	**panna fresca** sold in cartons
cream, whipped	**panna montata** sold in 200 gram packets
margarine	**margarina**
milk	**latte** sold in cartons of 1 litre, $\frac{1}{2}$ litre and sometimes $\frac{1}{4}$ litre. *Scremato* is skimmed milk; *intero* is full-cream
yoghurt	**yogurt**

Groceries

beans, dried	**fagioli**
beans, kidney	**borlotti** dried red haricot beans
beans, tuscan	**fagioli toscani** big fat white variety
breadcrumbs	**pane grattugiato** sold already prepared in packets
capers	**capperi**
chick peas	**ceci** small, yellow, round
cinnamon	**cannella** sold in sticks or powder
coffee	**caffé** a very wide selection of beans and ground coffee available, mostly prepacked: it is of high quality but correspondingly expensive
flour, maize	**polenta** yellow rich maize flour (a staple food of northern Italy)
flour, plain	**farina** wheat flour
lentils	**lenticchie**
mayonnaise	**maionese**
mineral water	**acqua minerale**
mushrooms, dried	**funghi** usually woodland mushrooms bought dried (**secchi**) in tiny packets. Very pungent and good in slow-cooked dishes
mustard	**mostarda**
nutmeg	**noce moscata** common spice in Italian cooking
oil, blended	**olio di semi vari**
oil, olive	**olio di oliva** three grades sold, usually in litre, or $\frac{1}{2}$ litre tins
oil, peanut	**olio di noce**
oil, sunflower	**olio di girasole**
pasta, dried	**pasta** the national dish of Italy: made from semolina, wheat flour and water.

An enriched version, **pasta all'uova**, contains eggs. Pasta comes in nearly 200 different shapes and two colours, white and green. All pasta is numbered, the numbers being standard to all proprietary brands of pasta. Some of the more common include:

lasagne (1) large, flat; either white or green **verde**

tagliatelle (4–7) long, flat strips

vermicelli (13–14) long, thin, and hollow

spaghetti (15)

penne (18–24) short, hollow pieces

gnocchi (26–27) little corrugated shells

fusilli (28) short, flat and twisted

rigatoni (31) short, curved and hollow

semi di mellone (61) tiny, like long-grained rice

farfalle (66) literally 'butterflies'

nidi (101–104) like a bird's nest

pasta, fresh	fresh pasta is soft and needs to be eaten soon after it is bought. As well as plain pastas, there is **ravioli**, fresh pasta squares filled with meat or **ricotta** cheese and spinach (cook in broth; or in water to serve with tomato sauce)
pine nuts	**pignoli** oval-shaped kernels of pine cones
pepper	**pepe** either powdered or peppercorns
pepper, cayenne	**pepe cayenne**
raisins	**uva secca**
rice	**riso** grown in the north of Italy, and widely used throughout the country
salt	**sale** sea salt or crystal best – well worth extra price. Bought at tobacconists, since salt and tobacco are both state monopolies. Look for blue and white '*Sale e Tabacchi*' sign, or simply large T
sugar	**zucchero**
sultanas	**uva passa**
tea	**té** not an Italian drink but some brands imported
toothpicks	**stecchini**
vanilla	**vaniglia** sold in black pods, loose or packaged
vinegar, wine	**aceto di vino**

The Bakery **La Panetteria, Il Panificio**

Bread, *pane* in Italy, is sold by the kilo, but as loaves tend to be much the same size they are really charged by the loaf, the half loaf, or even the slice. The standard bread is often called 'Tipo O' (from the class of flour), and often there is a slightly more expensive alternative. Bread varies from region to region greatly.

bread roll	**panino**, plural **panini**
brown bread	**pane nero** common in the north
French bread	**filone di pane** long, thin and crusty
soft crust roll	**panino all'olio**
wholemeal bread	**pane integrale, pane di casa** literally 'home bread' – wholesome and keeps well

The Ice Cream Shop   **La Gelateria**
The Pastry Shop   **La Pasticceria**

Italy is world famous for her ice cream *gelati* – a reputation richly deserved for the ingenuity of flavours, and the richness of taste is incomparable. Ice cream is sold in cornets *cornetta*, small or large, or in tubs, which come in many sizes.

The pastry shop *la pasticceria* is more often than not a part of the *gelateria*. The choice of pastries and cakes is usually endless, with the speciality of the region being most evident. However, there are a few that are common throughout Italy:

biscuits	**biscotti**
brioche	**brioche alla panna**
cake	**torte**
croissant	**cornetti**
danish pastry	**danesi**
doughnut	**craffen**
eclairs	**bigné alla crema**
fruit tart	**crostata**
mille-feuilles	**diplomatici**
rum baba	**baba al rum**
swiss roll	**cannoli**

The Greengrocer   **La Verdoleria**

'I'm 60 years old', an old woman told me in a Rome street market, 'I got up at 4 o'clock to have everything looking nice for you. I hope you appreciate my stall!' In common with most fruit and vegetable stalls throughout Italy, it was colourful and attractively laid out with fresh local produce on a bed of bracken. Everything is sold by the kilo unless marked by the piece, *l'uno*, or if expensive by *il etto* 100 gram.

Vegetables	**Legumi**
artichokes	**carciofi** sold *l'uno* (the one). Common and inexpensive vegetable with tough spiky green/purple overlapping leaves
asparagus	**asparagi** sold by the bunch in spring and early summer. Usually expensive; wild asparagus, which is darker green and smaller, particularly so

aubergine or egg plant	**melanzane** one of the most common vegetables in Italy. Usually large, purple and shiny and oval in shape, but can be white and small like an egg (from whence it derives its name)
basil, sweet	**basilico** bought by the bunch (and sometimes given away with a large order). A leaf herb, bright green, oval-shaped leaf with sweet aromatic scent. A basis for much Italian cookery – especially good in tomato dishes. It does not dry well, so always try to buy it fresh
bay leaves	**lauro** an essential leaf herb in Italian cuisine. Bitter scented, usually given away or charged at a few lire for a sprig
beans, broad	**fave** fairly plentiful throughout the year
beans, french	**fagiolini** common throughout Italy; sometimes white, more often light green
beans, runner	**fagiole coralo** not very common
beetroot	**barbabietola**
broccoli	**broccoli** inexpensive when in season (spring or summer)
cabbage	**cavolo**
carrots	**carote**
cauliflower	**cavolfiori** sold *l'uno* (by the piece), but charged by the kilo
celery	**sedano** a basic ingredient for all Italian soups, sold all year round. Often sold in *verdura per minestrone* – chopped vegetables ready prepared for minestrone
courgettes or baby marrow	**zucchini** often sold with orange–yellow flower
cucumber	**cetriolo** sold *l'uno* by the piece
endive	**cicoria** pale yellow, frizzy leaves. Slightly bitter flavour
fennel	**finocchio** light green–white bulbous stem with strong aniseed flavour and scent. Widely used cooked or raw (*finocchio* is also the Italian slang for a homosexual)

garlic	**aglio** sold by the *testa* (the head)
juniper	**ginepro** only the berries used. Sold in sprigs
leeks	**porri**
lettuce	**lattuga** varieties include: **capuccina** – round and open with a heart; **grande** with long dark green leaves like a cos; **radicchio rosso** – red lettuce. Everything else is called just *insalata*
marjoram, sweet	**maggiorana** one of the best leaf herbs and much used in Italian cookery
mint	**menta** common and usually given away. **Menta Romana** is peppermint
myrtle	**mirto** common herb–sprigs given or sold for a few lire
mushrooms	**funghi** now all cultivated; large, dirty brown button variety sold by the *etto* (or use *funghi secchi*, page 142)
onions	**cipolle**
onions, spring	**cipolline** don't confuse with **aglio fresco** (fresh garlic), which is very much stronger
oregano	**oregano** sometimes sold fresh, but more often dried
parsley	**prezzemolo** small, flat serrated leaf with long stalk. Sold by the bunch
peas	**piselli**
peppers	**peperoni** three colours: red, yellow **peperoni gialli** and green **peperoni verdi**. Choose larger for stuffing, smaller for frying. The redder the pepper the hotter
radishes	**radicchi** round **tondi** or long **ravanelli**

rosemary	**rosmarino** strong dominant herb sold for a few lire, but usually sprigs given away
sage	**salvia** not uncommon small heart-shaped leaf herb
spinach	**spinaci** dark green leaf with short stem, usually sold with roots attached
Swiss chard	**bietola** similar to spinach with lighter green leaves and thick white edible stalks
tomatoes	**pomodori** grown all over Italy, especially the south. Plentiful and cheap. Large, craggy and round for salad – the smaller plum variety is usually sold for preserving and cooking. Available most of the year. Out of season use canned or *concentrato* (tomato puree)
turnips	**rapa**

The Fruiterer Il Fruttivendolo

Fruit	**Frutta**
almonds	**mandorle** cheap and plentiful, available fresh from May until Christmas
apples	**mele** sold throughout the year. The best red apples are **delizioni**, the best yellow **ranette**
apricots	**albicocche** deep yellow flesh and skin. Early fruit, very expensive and thus sold by the *etto*
cherries	**ciliegi** plentiful and cheap throughout their long season (early summer to autumn)
chestnuts	**castagne** widely used in the north of Italy, also in ice creams and confectionery
figs	**fichi** cheap and plentiful from September onwards
grapes	**uva** dessert grapes are usually white. Cheap in season (mid-summer onwards) and wonderfully good
grapefruit	**pompelmo** sold in packets of three

lemons	**limoni** very cheap and plentiful, particularly in the south where they are somewhat sweeter, **cedri**. Green lemons tend to be sourer than yellow
loquats or medlars	**nespole** small but succulent orange-skinned fruit sometimes with brown blotches, the orange flesh has two or three pips. Good eating and cheap all through the summer
melon	**melone** several varieties sold throughout the year, most are locally grown but some are now imported
melon, water	**cocomero** vast dark-green skinned, red-fleshed fruit with black pips they are usually sold by the piece and charged by the kilo. Very cheap all through the summer; often sold off lorries at the side of the road
oranges	**arance** cheap and plentiful throughout the summer

Fruit & Vegetables

sanguigne blood oranges have a red/orange skin and red succulent flesh. Good for pressing or eating whole.

vaniglie vanilla oranges from Sicily

peaches **pesche** very cheap and plentiful throughout the summer

pears **pere**

pineapple **ananasso** imported, good but expensive

plums **susine, prugne** deep purple in colour they are expensive in early summer but very cheap thereafter

strawberries **fragole** quite expensive in the spring but cheaper as the season progresses. Wild strawberries, *nemi*, are the best but always expensive

walnuts **noci** late autumn season; they are mainly used in ice cream and confectionery

Wines and Spirits

Wines

Italian wine used to be thought inferior to all French wine. Today, the stricter government and self-imposed controls of origin, quality, quantity and age have improved Italian wine until it rivals many of the noble French vintages. The freshness of the white wine, or the lightness of the red, goes well with the fine Italian cooking.

The *vino da tavola* (the wine of the region) either white *bianco*, red *rosso*, or rosé *rosato*, is good. Some (particularly some from the north) are better than others (from the south), and so it is fortunate that all the wines are generally available all over Italy.

Taking each region separately here are some of the better-known wines:

Piedmont (around Turin) some of Italy's best red wines come from this region such as *Barolo* and *Barbaresco* with the rather fruity *Grignolino*. It is the home of the sparkling *Asti Spumante* and all the vermouths. *Gavi Bianco* is a good light dry white wine from *Cortei*

Liguria (around Genoa) a region of good white wines like *Cinqueterre* and *Coronata*

Veneto (around Venice) the well-known *Soave* comes from here – a fresh white wine often found in England as the *vino di casa* (house white). *Valpolicella*, a red wine, is probably better drunk chilled

Emilia-Romagna (around Reggio Emilia). *Lambrusco* is a curious fizzy red wine which is good, as is the *Albana* and the more common *Sangiovese*

Tuscany (between Florence and Siena) is *Chianti*, sold either in the classic straw-covered *fiasco* or a conventional bottle. *Chianti Classico*, is the best. *Chianti* is a distinctive wine with quite a strong earthy flavour to both red and white

Umbria (between Florence and Rome) *Orvieto* produces a very palatable white wine while opposite on the Adriatic coast *Verdicchio*, in a green bottle shaped like a curvacious woman, is a fine white!

Lazio (around Rome) *Est! Est! Est!*, a rather sweet white wine, has a more remarkable name than quality. The fragrant, dry *Frascati* also comes from this region

Compania (around and below Naples) the slopes of the volcano Vesuvius provide *Lacrima Christi* 'the tears of Christ'. All things to all men – either red or white, sweet or dry, they all have a distinct flavour of the minerals from the volcano. Down the coast *Ravello* has white, red and rosé

Sicily is probably best known for the fortified wine *Marsala* but *Monte Etna* is a good white wine and slightly better than the *Corvo* of Palermo

Aperitifs
Italians drink their vermouths (*bianco, rosso,* or *rosato*) before a meal as their *aperitivo*. *Martini, Cinzano* and *Campari* are as well-known in England as they are in their native land. But you will also find a

great many unfamiliar ones. *Gancia* and *Bianco Sarti* are especially good. For those mornings after the night before *Fernet Branca* is good.

Spirits
Italian brandy is not especially notable: *Stock* and *Vecchia Romagna* are perhaps the best of them. *Grappa* is an acrid liqueur made from grape pressings and a personal favourite. Every Italian bar has a vast range of liqueurs drunk as *digestivi* after the meal. They are made with every likely fruit (the label has a picture of which) or herb – a few are *Nocino* (made with nuts), *Sambucca* (aniseed), *Cent'erbe* (literally 'a hundred herbs', in many different varieties, mostly mint-flavoured), and *Aurum* (orange-flavoured) – and some unlikely ones: *Latte di suocera* ('mother-in-law's milk'!) is herbal and very fierce. Try glasses of liqueurs in a bar before committing yourself to a bottle.

COOKING

Italian cooking with the endless invasions from the time of the ancient Greeks and Romans has continued to grow and change throughout the centuries. The south, overrun many times by very different races (Spanish, Arabs, French and Swabians – from part of Germany), has adopted a little of each to make up its own original cuisine. The great trading cities of Venice and Genoa added oriental spices and dishes to their cuisine, while in the Renaissance period cooking was developed as an art like painting and sculpture, and patronized by princes and the rich.

Despite the unification of Italy in the last century, true Italian cookery has remained regional. Dishes like the ubiquitous *pasta* and *pizza* do stray to other parts, but you will still find the best *pizza* in Naples, its home, as you will find the best risottos in Lombardy, the best pork in Bologna, the finest meats in Tuscany and the best lamb from the spiritual home of Italian cooking, Rome. *Buon appetito!*

Minestrone

This famous Italian soup must not be confused with the thin watery substance served up in England under the same name, or with *Minestre*, which is a *thin* Italian soup.

Minestrone is thick and robust, the best part of a meal in itself. Ask the greengrocer for *verdura per minestrone* (vegetables already chopped). I have given quantities enough for 8, as this soup reheats well. You can vary the ingredients according to what is available – the important thing is the large quantity and variety of vegetables.

125 g/4 oz dried kidney beans	*1 potato, diced*
50 g/2 oz dried chick peas	*1 small or ¼ large cabbage, finely*
4 tablespoons olive oil	*shredded*
2 medium onions, chopped	*4 celery stalks, finely sliced*
175 g/6 oz salt pork, cubed	*125 g/4 oz pasta – any small kind,*
2 cloves garlic, crushed	*macaroni, or broken-up spaghetti*
6 tomatoes, chopped	*225 g/8 oz peas*
herbs — oregano, thyme or basil	*100 g/4 oz grana cheese (such as*
2¹/₂ litres/4 pts chicken stock	*Parmesan), grated*
4 carrots, chopped	

Soak the kidney beans and chick peas overnight.

Heat the olive oil in a large saucepan and soften the onions. Add the salt pork, garlic, tomatoes, herbs and a little of the stock. Cook a little and stir well. Add the kidney beans and chick peas, then put in the rest of the stock. Cover and simmer gently for 1½ hours.

Add the remaining vegetables and pasta so they are all cooked – but still firm – at the same time. With these ingredients: add the carrots and potato, simmer for about 10 minutes; add the cabbage, celery and pasta, simmer for 5 minutes; finally add the peas and simmer for not more than 10 minutes.

Just before serving stir in half the cheese. Serve in large soup bowls sprinkled with the rest of the cheese.

Minestra di cicoria   Endive soup

Endive is not quite the right translation as *cicoria* is not seen in England. Whatever the true translation, it does make a fine soup.

2 kg/4¹/₂ lb cicoria
2 tablespoons olive oil
3 or 4 cloves garlic
2 slices bread

1¹/₂ litres/2¹/₂ pints stock (chicken is best)
50 g/2 oz grana cheese (such as Parmesan)

Boil the *cicoria* in salted water for just 1 minute, then drain and chop coarsely.

Heat the oil in a pan with the garlic. Cut the bread into small squares and fry until golden-brown *croutons*. Remove these, drain and keep warm.

When garlic is just changing colour as it cooks, add the *cicoria* and stir. Add the chicken stock and simmer for half an hour.

Remove the garlic. Season with salt and pepper and stir in the cheese. Scatter with the *croutons* and serve.

Salsa al pomodoro   Tomato sauce (in Spain called *Salsa de tomate*)

Two countries, one sauce – used in dozens of dishes. These quantities make about 500 g/1 lb of sauce, or a little more. Another Italian name for a plain tomato sauce is *sugo di pomodori*, or just *sugo*.

1 onion, chopped
1 kg/2 lb tomatoes

2 tablespoons olive oil
fresh basil or parsley

Heat the oil in a large pan and cook the onion until golden brown. Add the tomatoes and herb, and simmer on a low heat for about half an hour. As the sauce thickens, season with salt and pepper.

If you want a smooth sauce without seeds or skins, rub the sauce through a sieve when it has cooked.

The Spanish add a very small chopped red pepper.

Pasta

Pasta (*pasta asciutta*) is synonymous with Italy. Despite the hundreds of different sizes and shapes it is moulded into, the method of cooking is the same; only the sauces change. In the south of Italy it is rare to start the meal without some form of pasta. Allow about 125 g/4 oz per person. Serve grated *grana* cheese to sprinkle over each plateful.

To cook pasta

Always use the largest saucepan available (if you cook pasta in too little water it sticks and turns into a glutinous mess). Fill nearly to the brim with water, add a tablespoonful of oil and a liberal amount of salt. When it is boiling hard, and the oil has mixed with the water, add the pasta.

Thick forms of dried pasta need to be cooked for about 10 or 12 minutes, thin forms like *vermicelli* for only 5 or 7. Fresh pasta cooks in a shorter time. Pasta should be cooked *al dente*, that is, slightly chewy. A good test is to remove a piece and squeeze it. If it breaks easily, the pasta is cooked. Drain by pouring into a colander or sieve.

Return to the hot saucepan and add 2 tablespoons of whatever sauce you have chosen. Mix well. Put pasta in a warm serving dish, then put the sauce on top and mix. Somehow doing the mixing in two stages achieves a better result.

Spaghetti al pomodoro   Spaghetti with tomato sauce

Of all the thousands of pasta dishes, this simple and truly Neapolitan dish is perhaps the best. Enough for 4.

2 tablespoons olive oil
1 small onion, finely chopped
1 kg/2¹/₄ lb tomatoes, chopped; skinned and seeded if you wish
basil, chopped
600 g/1¹/₄ lb spaghetti
50 g/2 oz grana *cheese (such as Parmesan), grated*

Heat the olive oil in a pan and cook the onions until soft brown. Add the tomatoes and basil and simmer for a good ½ hour. When the sauce begins to thicken season with salt and a little pepper.

Meanwhile cook the spaghetti. When it is cooked, drain, mix with the sauce, and serve immediately. Serve the *grana* in a separate bowl to sprinkle over it.

Spaghetti alle vongole   Spaghetti with clams

Seen on all Italian menus, but even more delicious prepared in your own kitchen. You can buy the *vongole* canned, but they are much better fresh. This is one of the few pasta dishes which is eaten without any *grana* cheese sprinkled on it. Serves 4.

5 tablespoons olive oil	*2 kg/4 lb well-washed* vongole
6 cloves garlic, 4 whole and 2	*(carpet shells)*
crushed	*parsley, finely chopped*
	600 g/1¹/₄ lb spaghetti

Heat half the olive oil in a large saucepan and cook the whole cloves of garlic until they turn golden brown. Discard the garlic.

Add all the clams and cook with the lid on for a few minutes, shaking well, until they open. Strain off the liquid but do not throw it away. Remove the clams from their shells, keeping a few shells for decoration. *Discard any clams that have not opened.*

Heat the remaining olive oil in a pan, add the crushed garlic and liquid drained off the clams. Season well with pepper and cook for 2 minutes. Add the clams.

Meanwhile cook the spaghetti. Add the clam sauce and serve immediately, decorating with shells.

Penne all'Arrabbiata   Angry pens

Penne are short thick pasta, cut obliquely so they look a little like the end of a quill pen (but you can use another shape of pasta). The anger is from the heat of the chillies in this dish from Abruzzi, a region known for its hot food. Enough for 4.

3 tablespoons olive oil	*2 or 3 hot chilli peppers, preferably*
2 cloves garlic, chopped	*fresh but dried will do; seeded*
4 large or 6 smaller tomatoes,	*and finely chopped*
chopped	*500 g/1 lb penne (or other pasta)*
fresh basil, chopped	*100 g/4 oz* grana *cheese* (pecorino
	is particularly appropriate)

Heat the oil in a pan and cook the garlic until transparent. Add the tomatoes, basil, chilli peppers, salt and pepper. Simmer for 15 minutes or until the sauce thickens.

Meanwhile cook the *penne*.

Mix the sauce with the *penne* and serve immediately, with the *grana* in a separate bowl to sprinkle over.

Vermicelli alla puttanesca   Whores vermicelli

Perhaps it is the hot chilli that gives this fine sauce its name; she will accommodate 6 people!

5 tablespoons olive oil
3 or 4 cloves garlic
500 g/1 lb tomatoes
100 g/3¹/₂ oz capers, drained
200 g/7 oz black olives, stoned

1 hot chilli, chopped very fine (use
more than one if you like it
hotter)
1 tablespoon fresh oregano, chopped
750 g/1³/₄ lb vermicelli
150 g/5 oz grana *cheese (such as*
Parmesan)

Heat the oil in a pan and add the garlic. When golden in colour, discard the garlic. Add the tomatoes and simmer for about ½ hour until the sauce thickens. Season with salt and pepper. Add the capers, olives, chilli and oregano.

Meanwhile boil the *vermicelli* – number 5 only takes 5 minutes (page 155).

Mix the sauce with the *vermicelli* and serve immediately, with the *grana* in a separate bowl to sprinkle over.

Pasta al olio e aglio

A robust and rustic dish – if you like oil and garlic! These quantities are for 4.

500 g/1 lb pasta
olive oil
5 cloves garlic, crushed – or rather
more, according to your taste

150 g/5 oz grana *cheese (*pecorino
is especially good for this dish),
grated

Cook the pasta in plenty of salted water. Meanwhile cook the garlic gently in a little olive oil, until transparent.

When the pasta is cooked, drain it and return to the saucepan (off the heat). Add the garlic in its oil, and mix, adding more oil until every strand or piece of pasta is throughly coated. Serve immediately sprinkled with plenty of cheese.

Rosemary in moderation is a useful addition.

Spaghetti alla carbonara   Spaghetti with egg and bacon

No tomatoes in this pasta sauce! Enough for 4.

500 g/1 lb spaghetti
50 g/2 oz butter (or use oil)
100 g/4 oz bacon or ham
   (prosciutto *or* coppa)

¹/₂ small carton thick cream
3 eggs
125 g/4¹/₂ oz grana *cheese (such as*
   Parmesan), grated oregano

Cook the spaghetti.

Meanwhile melt half the butter in a pan and add chopped bacon. Fry until crisp. Remove from heat, and stir in the cream when cooled a little. Put into a hot serving dish.

Beat the eggs with half the *grana*; season with salt, pepper and a little oregano.

Drain the spaghetti. Immediately put it in the serving dish and pour the egg mixture over. Mix well. The egg cooks in the heat of the spaghetti and 'sets'.

Serve immediately, scattering the rest of the *grana* on each plateful.

Lasagne al forno   Baked *lasagne*

One of the great dishes of Italy. The Italian housewife makes her own pasta, but this is a needless luxury as the *lasagne* in the shops is excellent. Buy the *lasagne* fresh rather than dried if you can. *Lasagne verde* (coloured green with spinach) is colourful and more tasty than the plain variety.

4 tablespoons olive oil
1 onion, sliced
750 g/1¹/₂ lb minced meat,
   preferably lean beef
2 cloves garlic, crushed
1 teaspoon sugar
4 large tomatoes, chopped

¹/₂ litre/1 pint béchamel sauce (page
   204)
nutmeg
500 g/1 lb lasagne
100 g/3¹/₂ oz grana *cheese (such as*
   Parmesan), grated

Heat 2 tablespoons of olive oil in a pan and cook the onions until golden. Add the meat, garlic, sugar and a little pepper. When the meat has sealed add the tomatoes, a sprinkle of salt and a little water. Cook gently for 15 minutes.

Meanwhile make the béchamel sauce, and grate some nutmeg into it.

Take the largest saucepan available, and boil salted water in it. Add a tablespoon of oil and add the *lasagne* sheet by sheet, stirring carefully so the sheets do not stick together. Boil dried *lasagne* for about 12 minutes, fresh for 5. Remove the *lasagne* carefully, laying each sheet separately on a flat surface.

Oil a large oven-proof dish, and put a layer of *lasagne* on the bottom. Cover with a layer of meat sauce, then a sprinkling of *grana*, then a layer of béchamel sauce, followed by another layer of *lasagne*, and so on. End with a layer of béchamel sprinkled with *grana*.

Bake in a moderate oven for 30 minutes, or until the top has turned golden.

Serve immediately.

Pappa al pomodoro fresco   Pap with fresh tomatoes

Curious, very simple and good. All quantities (given here for 6) are rather vague, and depend on how much you want it to taste of garlic and of tomatoes! Serve as a starter.

*stale white bread, perhaps
    750 g/1³/₄ lb
3 to 5 cloves garlic, depending on
    your taste, crushed*

*4 tablespoons olive oil
400 g/14 oz tomatoes, skinned
good bunch fresh basil, chopped*

Soak the bread in water for ½ hour or so, and squeeze out. Meanwhile cook the garlic gently in the oil, add the skinned tomatoes and basil. Heat through, add the bread, stir until thoroughly hot and serve.

Mozzarella in carrozza

Originally a Neapolitan dish, as in Naples a *carrozza* (carriage) was everybody's dream. Here is a 'dream' way of eating this superlative cheese.

*for each one
50 g/2 oz mozzarella cheese, sliced
2 slices white bread
2 tablespoons olive oil*

*batter (these quantities make
    enough for 4)
3 eggs
1 wineglass milk
a little flour*

Make a tight sandwich with the bread and cheese. Cut off the crusts.

Make the batter by beating eggs and milk together. Season with salt and pepper. Sprinkle flour over sandwich and immerse in the batter, and leave it to soak up the batter.

Heat the oil and fry sandwiches until golden on both sides. Eat immediately.

Fagioli al forno   Tuscan beans

Popular in the month of July, Tuscan beans are wholesome and cheap. Useful as a vegetable with meat, or cold with vinaigrette.

500 g/1 lb Tuscan beans or white haricot beans
2 cloves garlic, crushed
fresh basil, chopped coarsely
225 g/8 oz belly of pork

Soak the beans overnight.

Put all the ingredients into an oven dish and cover with water. Cover the dish and bake in a slow oven for 3 to 3½ hours.

Drain before serving.

Lenticchie verdi con salsicce   Green lentils with sausages

Green lentils are so good that they are rarely seen outside Italy. Make the most of them with the Italians' equally fine spiced sausages. The recipe serves 4.

350 g/12 oz green lentils
½ kg/1 lb spiced sausages (about 6)
1 litre/1³/4 pints stock (chicken is best)
½ kg/1 lb tomatoes, chopped
1 clove garlic, crushed
parsley, finely chopped

Pick the lentils over for any bits of grit or grass and soak well covered in water overnight.

Put all the ingredients into a large saucepan, making sure the sausages are well buried in the lentils. Bring to the boil, reduce heat, cover and simmer gently for 1 hour. Strain off any excess liquid and serve with plenty of fresh bread.

Parmigiana di melanzane   Aubergine pie

This imaginative recipe is one of the simple delights of Italy. The tomato sauce is optional, but to my mind essential. These quantities make a main course for 4, or a starter for 6.

1 kg/2¹/₄ lb aubergines
¹/₂ wineglass oil
1 kg/2¹/₄ lb tomatoes, chopped
good bunch fresh basil

300 g/11 oz mozzarella *cheese,*
   thinly sliced
100 g/4 oz grana *cheese (such as*
   Parmesan), grated

Cut the aubergines into slices and sprinkle liberally with salt to 'sweat' out the bitter moisture. Leave for at least 3 hours.

Rinse and dry the aubergines carefully. Heat the oil in a pan and cook the aubergines until tender (about 10 minutes). Remove and drain.

Make a tomato sauce by cooking the tomatoes with the basil, seasoned with salt and pepper. (Don't forget to remove the tomato skins if you don't like them.)

Cover the bottom of an oven-proof dish with aubergine slices, then build up in layers, alternating aubergines, *mozzarella* and tomato sauce, and sprinkling with *grana* and a little salt and pepper. End with a layer of tomato sauce with *grana* sprinkled on top.

Bake in a fairly hot oven for ½ hour and serve immediately.

Uova al pomodoro   Eggs with tomato

This Neapolitan dish is known as 'Eggs in hell', despite its divine taste. Serves 4.

700 g/1¹/₄ lb tomatoes
2 tablespoons olive oil
1 onion, chopped

1 clove garlic, crushed
basil, finely chopped
4 eggs

Peel the tomatoes. (Pour boiling water over them and leave for a few minutes; the skins then slip easily off.) Heat the oil in a pan, and cook the onion and garlic until soft brown. Add the tomatoes and basil. Simmer until the sauce thickens. Season with salt and pepper.

Make four indentations in the sauce, and break an egg into each. Cook until the egg whites are set.

Serve instantly with plenty of fresh bread.

Insalata di mozzarella e pomodori   Mozzarella and tomato salad

A very superior salad made with the simplest ingredients for a lucky 6 people.

½ kg/1 lb tomatoes (for salads the round, craggy variety are better than the small, plum-shaped type)

225 g/8 oz mozzarella *cheese*
1 wineglass vinaigrette (page 204)
basil

Slice the tomatoes and cheese thinly. Arrange attractively on a plate and sprinkle with vinaigrette. Serve with fresh basil chopped over each plate.

The salad is marginally improved if chilled before serving.

A useful addition to this salad is a peeled and sliced avocado, or some salami slices mixed with the *mozzarella*.

Insalata di rinforzo   Reinforced salad!

An excellent Neapolitan salad, worthy of its name!

1 medium cauliflower
125 g/2 oz capers (drained of vinegar)
12 black olives, stoned

1 green pepper
1 red pepper
1 wineglass vinaigrette

Quarter the cauliflower and boil it in salted water for only 5 minutes, so that it is still quite hard. Remove and drain.

Cut the tops off the peppers and remove the core and seeds. Slice finely. Put the peppers, capers, olives and cauliflower into a bowl. Pour over the vinaigrette, turn and leave for at least 1 hour – preferably in the refrigerator.

Serve with plenty of white bread.

Insalata di pesce spada   Swordfish with a piquant tomato sauce

There is great activity in a seaside village when swordfish are caught – understandably, as it is perhaps the best of Mediterranean fish. It seems expensive, but there is little waste. More common than swordfish is tunny, which is almost as good. Enough for 4.

2 tablespoons olive oil	*12 black olives*
4 swordfish (or tunny) steaks	*good pinch cayenne pepper*
500 g/1 lb tomato sauce (page 154)	*fresh basil, chopped*

Heat the oil in a pan and lightly fry the steaks. Depending on their thickness, they will need around 5 minutes each side – until they are barely cooked through.

Add the tomato sauce mixed with the olives, cayenne and basil, and simmer uncovered for 15 minutes.

Serve with rice and a green salad.

Sarde a beccaficcu   Sardines *beccaficcu*

Beccaficcu are figpeckers, little birds which like larks, blackbirds and thrushes are, alas, an Italian delicacy. In this Sicilian dish the sardines end up looking like figpeckers, hence the name.

1 kg/2 lb fresh sardines	*1 egg*
1 small onion, finely chopped	*50 g/2 oz pine nuts*
juice of ¹/₂ lemon	*12 black olives, stoned and chopped*
2 cloves garlic, crushed	*50 g/2 oz capers, drained*
3 thick slices white bread without	*50 g/2 oz sultanas*
* crusts, crumbled*	*about 1 tablespoon olive oil*

Clean and gut the sardines. Cut the heads off, but leave the tails on. Remove the backbones, if you can do this tricky job neatly.

Mix together the onion, lemon juice, garlic, crumbled bread, egg, pine nuts, olives, capers and sultanas into a stuffing. Lay out each sardine on its back and fill with stuffing. If you have taken the backbones out you can roll the fish up towards the tail. Otherwise place them side by side in an oven-proof dish. Pour a little olive oil over the fish and bake in a hot oven for 10 minutes.

Serve immediately with plenty of fresh bread.

Alici ammollicate   Fresh anchovies *au gratin*

This fine little fish cooked in a Neapolitan way is a special treat.
This is also a good recipe for sardines. Enough for 6.

1 kg/2 1/4 lb fresh anchovies   *4 tablespoons breadcrumbs*
150 ml/1/4 pt olive oil   *3 tablespoons oregano, chopped*
2 cloves garlic, chopped

Gut the anchovies and remove the heads and tails. (Take out the
backbones too, if you can do this tricky job.) Wash them
thoroughly. Place in a shallow oven-proof dish and sprinkle on half
the olive oil. Mix the breadcrumbs, oregano and remaining olive
oil, and put this mixture over the anchovies.

Bake in a hot oven for 15 minutes.

Serve hot with potatoes.

Dentice ripiena   Stuffed dentex

A fine stuffing worthy of the delicate flavour of the dentex. You can
adapt the recipe to other large fish, such as John Dory (*pesce San
Pietro*).

stuffing

1 dentex, about 1 kg/2 1/4 lb   *3 thick slices bread*
150 ml/1 1/4 pint olive oil   *1/2 glass white wine*
juice of 1 lemon   *100 g/3 1/2 oz cooked rice*
2 tablespoons oregano, chopped   *1 small pear, peeled, cored and*
30 g/1 oz butter   *mashed to a puree*
wooden toothpicks or cocktail sticks   *1 onion, chopped finely*
                                         parsley
                                         1 egg

Clean and wash the fish, removing the tail and the head (if you are
squeamish). Marinate in the oil, lemon juice and oregano for about
½ hour. Remove the crusts and crumble the bread into crumbs.
Soak half of them in the wine. Mix the rice, pear, onion and parsley
together and bind with the egg. Season with salt and pepper. Pour
off the marinade and stuff the dentex with this mixture, closing it
with toothpicks.

Return the fish to its dish, dot it with the butter and sprinkle with
salt. Put in a hot oven.

After a few minutes, when the butter has melted, sprinkle the
fish with breadcrumbs. Bake for about another 20 minutes –
depending on the size of the fish – basting occasionally.

Serve with rice and a tomato salad.

Calamaro ripieno   Stuffed squid

Anyone squeamish about eating squid will be missing out on this tasty Italian dish. This makes enough for 6.

6 medium squid	*100 g/3¹/₂oz black olives, stoned*
2 or 3 cloves garlic	*and chopped*
¹/₂ wineglass olive oil	*500 g/1 lb tomato sauce (page 154)*
50 g/2 oz breadcrumbs	*2 sprigs of parsley, finely chopped*
50 g/2 oz capers	

Wash the squid thoroughly in cold water. Cut off the tentacles and chop finely.

Heat the oil in a pan and add the whole garlic. Cook until they begin to take on colour. Add the breadcrumbs, capers, olives and squid tentacles. Allow to cook for 5 minutes, then add half the parsley. Allow to cool.

Stuff the squid bodies with the mixture (not too full, as the stuffing will swell in the cooking), and place in an oven-proof dish. Cover with the tomato sauce and bake in a moderate oven for an hour.

Sprinkle the remaining parsley on top before serving.

Bracioluce di maiale   Stuffed leg of pork

This recipe comes from the Campania of southern Italy, and is prepared as a celebration for the 'pork season'. It serves 6.

1¹/₄ kg/2¹/₂lb boned leg of pork	stuffing
50 g/2 oz butter	*150 g/6 oz chopped ham*
1 medium onion, chopped	*(prosciutto or use the cheaper*
1 glass red wine	*coppa)*
500 g/1 lb tomato sauce (page 154)	*200 g/7¹/₂oz minced meat*
	1 egg
	150 g/6 oz grana cheese (such as
	Parmesan), grated
	50 g/2 oz pine nuts
	50 g/2 oz raisins

Cut the leg of pork open (not all the way through) and salt on both sides. Mix all the stuffing ingredients together and season with salt and pepper. Spread the stuffing over the meat and truss it up with string.

Melt the butter in a pan and cook the onion until soft brown. Brown the meat on all sides, then add the wine. Cook until the wine has evaporated, then transfer the meat and onion to an oven-proof dish. Cover with the tomato sauce and cook in a moderate oven for about 1 hour.

Carve the joint – not too thinly or the stuffing will fall out. Serve with potatoes and a green vegetable.

Saltimbocca   Veal with ham and sage

Saltimbocca means 'jump in the mouth', an apt name for this classic Roman dish. Serves 4.

4 veal escalopes (pounded thin)	*50 g/2 oz butter*
juice of 1 lemon	*2 glasses dry white wine*
*4 slices ham (*prosciutto *or*	*sage, chopped fine*
coppa*)*	*wooden toothpicks or cocktail sticks*

Lay escalopes flat and sprinkle with the lemon juice, salt and a little pepper. Lay a slice of ham and a sprinkling of sage on each and roll up, securing with a toothpick.

Melt the butter in a pan and brown the veàl rolls on all sides. Pour in the wine. Allow to bubble for about 1 minute, then lower the heat and cover. Simmer until tender (between 10 and 15 minutes).

Serve with boiled new potatoes or a tomato salad.

Braciole al ragu   Beef olives

An interesting recipe that makes use of cheaper cuts of beef – shin (*muscolo*), leg (*moce*) or rump (*arosto*). A good meal for 6. The name is the only connection with olives.

12 thin slices of beef	stuffing
wooden toothpicks or cocktail sticks	*100 g/3 ¹/₂ oz ham (*prosciutto *or*
50 g/2 oz butter	coppa*), chopped*
1 medium onion, chopped	*2 cloves garlic, crushed*
1 glass red wine	*2 tablespoons breadcrumbs*
500 g/1 lb tomato sauce	*2 eggs*
	50 g/2 oz pine nuts
	2 tablespoons grated grana *cheese*
	(such as Parmesan)
	50 g/2 oz butter, cut into squares
	parsley, finely chopped

Mix all the ingredients for the stuffing until a smooth paste.

Flatten the pieces of beef by gently hammering with a wooden spoon. Place a little stuffing on each slice of beef and roll up, securing with a toothpick.

Melt butter in a pan. Cook the onion until it is soft brown, then fry the beef rolls on all sides. Add the wine and cook until it has evaporated. Add the tomato sauce and simmer covered for 30 minutes.

Serve piping hot with rice.

Osso bucco   Stewed veal knuckle

The traditional dish of Milan, now justly world famous. This is ample for 6. *Gremolada* is the special name for the mix of seasonings added just before serving.

1 kg/2 ¹/₄ lb veal knuckle (have the
  butcher saw it into slices
  7 cm/2¹/₂ in. thick)
flour seasoned with salt and pepper
50 g/2 oz butter
500 g/1 lb tomato sauce (page 154)
1 glass white wine

gremolada
1 clove garlic, crushed
parsley, chopped
rind of half a lemon, grated

Dip the veal in the seasoned flour. Melt the butter in a large pan. Arrange the veal slices on their sides so the marrow does not fall out during the cooking. Brown all over.

Mix the tomato sauce with the white wine and a pinch of sugar, and pour over the veal. Cover the pan and simmer gently for 2 hours, covered for the first hour, and uncovered for the second. The meat should then be almost falling off the bone.

Mix the *gremolada* ingredients together, add to the stew and cook for just a minute.

Serve immediately with rice.

Pollo tonnato   Chicken with tunny fish sauce

An admirable recipe mixing fish and fowl. Not difficult to prepare, this is a truly impressive dish. Enough for 4 hungry people, 6 if less hungry.

1 chicken (about 1¹/₂ kg/3¹/₂ lb)	*basil*
1 onion, sliced	*225 g/8 oz mayonnaise (page 204)*
1 carrot, sliced	*1 tin tunny (tuna) fish, about*
1 stick of celery, sliced	* 225 g/8 oz*

Put the chicken into a large saucepan with the onion, carrot, celery and basil. Bring just to the boil and simmer for at least 1 hour, until the chicken is tender and comes off the bone easily. Remove the saucepan from the heat and allow it to cool.

Meanwhile make the mayonnaise. Sieve or pound the tunny into a paste and mix with the mayonnaise. If it is very thick thin with a little cold chicken stock.

When chicken is cold, remove it from the stock (which you can use in another dish, such as Minestrone, page 153). Take the flesh off the carcass and mix with the tuna-mayonnaise sauce. Chill.

Serve with cooked rice moistened with vinaigrette.

Pollo alla diavola   Grilled chicken

. A common Tuscan way of preparing their excellent fat little chickens. Allow one small chicken (500–700 g/1–1½ lb) for 2 people.

chickens (have the butcher cut them	for each chicken
into halves, lengthways)	*5 tablespoons olive oil*
	juice of ¹/₂ lemon
	fresh oregano

Shake together the olive oil, lemon juice and oregano with a little salt and pepper. Rub half the mixture over the chicken.

Grill chicken over the embers of an open fire, sprinkling occasionally with the remaining oil and herb mixture.

Serve from the grill with green and tomato salads.

Zabaglione

As so often, this simplest of dishes is among the best.

for each person	*1 dessertspoonful sugar*
2 egg yolks	*3 tablespoons Marsala*

Beat the yolks and sugar together in a heat-proof bowl until they are stiff and pale yellow. Stir in the marsala.

Sit the bowl in a saucepan of hot water on a low flame. Stir or whisk the mixture all the time. As soon as it stiffens, take the bowl out of the saucepan instantly. Pour into glasses and serve.

Excellent with macaroons or any plain biscuits from the *pasticceria*.

Greece

SHOPPING

Shopping in Greece is always a surprise. Whereas most things are available in Athens and the larger towns (like fresh milk, recognizable cuts of meat and imported foodstuffs), the smaller villages and islands tend to be primitive, selling only what is in season, things that have just been caught or butchered that day, or dried and tinned foodstuffs. Then suddenly, it is a saint's day. From these basic shelves a whole new world of delicacies springs up – sweets and cakes, succulent baby lambs, kid and pork.

Each town and larger village has its own market, some trading daily (including Sundays), others once or twice a week. The Greeks like to see what they are buying and select it carefully. They expect you to do the same; to pick out the best tomatoes; to feel the fruit for ripeness. When it is very hot the butcher keeps his meat in a chill room and displays a list, somewhat exaggerated, of what is on offer. If you miss the fish market you may have a second chance to buy fish from a man on a bicycle pedalling round the village. In the smaller villages three-wheeler vans or small lorries come round with fruit and vegetables and a large brass balance, selling their wares at the end of a street. You will find shopping easy in Greece – a lemon seller is usually on the pavement outside the fish market, mounds of ripe tomatoes ready for stuffing on a trestle table near the butcher. You can find most things in Greece if you look for them or are prepared to accept a near-equivalent. The Greek lettering on the signs above the shops is confusing to visitors, and often to the Greeks as well, as the names of the shops are often spelt wrongly! More often the shops just have the name of the owner and his trade – 'Costas the butcher' ΚΩΣΤΑΣ Ο ΧΑΣΑΠΗΣ rather than 'butcher's shop' ΚΡΕΟΠΩΛΕΙΟΝ.

Here are a few phrases to help you on your way:

Good morning	**Kali mera**
Good afternoon	**Kali spera**
Please	**Parakalo**

Thank you	**Efharisto**
Please can I have ... kilos of...?	**Thelo ... kila yia ...**
That's too expensive	**Eenay poli akrivo**
A little more	**Pio akoma**
A little less	**Pio ligo**
Please will you cut it for me?	**Borite na to kopsete**
Please will you clean it for me?	**Tha to plenete**

1	**ena**
2	**thio**
3	**tria**
4	**tessera**
5	**pende**
6	**exi**
7	**efta**
8	**octo**
9	**ennya**
10	**theka**
100	**ekaton**

half	**misso**
quarter	**tetarto**
100 grams	**ekaton gramaticon**

The Fish Shop   **Echthiopolion** Εκδιοπολειον

Greece, with her serrated coastline and hundreds of islands, has been famous through the centuries for her fish, *psari*. Overfishing and the indiscriminate use of dynamite has sadly depleted her waters, and the consequent scarcity has made fish expensive, although the high demand ensures a rapid turnover of what is available, and fish is always fresh.

amberjack	**mayatico** large fish with dark blue back and yellow streak from cheek to tail
anchovy	**gávros** small fish with undershot jaw. Blue–black with silver sides. Caught on a waning moon
bass, sea	**lavraki** silver fish with grey–blue back. Excellent eating, firm flesh. Expensive

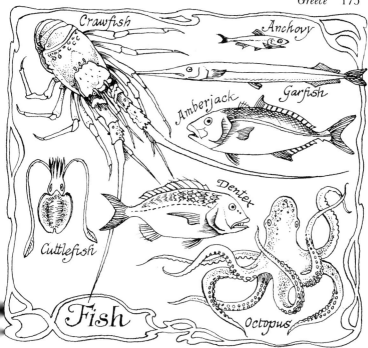

bonito	**palamida** common, fairly large fish of the mackerel family, and of a similar shape. Silver sides with distinctive longitudinal stripes slanting over a blue–green back
bream, gilt-head	**tsipoúra** easily recognized by golden spot on each cheek and golden crescent between the eyes
bream, red	**lithrini** reddish grey back with large black spot on shoulder
bream, sea	**fagrí** round fish with deep body. Silver–grey with pink fins and coarse scales
bream, Spanish	**moúsmouli** silver fish with large eyes and with definite black spot behind its cheek
crayfish	**astakos** larger than a lobster; has no claws but more meat, mostly in the tail. Brown in colour (red when cooked) with two long antennae. Quite common but expensive. Get up early or order one from the fishmonger the night before!

cuttlefish	**soupia** squat, oval creature with two long tentacles and eight short ones. Usually transparent-white, sometimes with zebra marks. Secretes sepia-coloured ink, hence its name
dentex	**synagrida** an admirable fish, rare and correspondingly expensive. Silver with steel-blue back, silver sides, and reddish tint to fins
Dublin Bay prawns	**karavida** miniature lobsters with outsized pincers. Rose-grey in colour. Not as good as they look
garfish	**zargana** common Greek fish and therefore inexpensive. Lethally sharp spiked beak on thin blue–green back, with silver body. Turquoise bones!
hake	**bacaliaros** silver–grey skin with long round slender body. Excellent eating with almost bone-free steaks, cutlets or whole
mackerel, horse or scad	**savridi** outsized eyes with giveaway stepped lateral line of lozenge-shaped scales on light greenish-blue back. Not specially good eating
mullet, grey	**kephalos** lead-coloured silver–grey striped fish with lighter underside and transparent membranes covering the eyes
mullet, red	**barbouni** rose coloured, common small fish. Has two barbules under its chin and yellowish stripes on its flank

mullet, thin-lipped grey	**mavráki** known in Greece as 'the gipsy' *yfto* because of its eating habits
mussels	**mydi** in Greece those sold are wild mussels, not cultivated
octopus	**octapous** the best variety are those with two rows of suckers on the tentacles
prawns	**garida** one name covers all the varieties of prawns, from small red, red with brown tints, to rose coloured. Sold by the kilo
sardines	**sardella** very common and inexpensive small fish with blue–green back, silver sides and belly. Available all year, although most plentiful May to September
sea perch	**sphyrida** grey or light grey, speckled with red on the back with distinctive white lines across the cheeks. Slender. Excellent eating
sole	**glossa** flat fish with brown or yellowish grey back, and white front. Quite common, good eating but expensive. Ask the fishmonger to fillet them if required
sprat	**papalina** tiny, silvery-scaled fish similar but inferior to the anchovy. Clean by pressing entrails out through slit behind the gills. The very small fry are sold as whitebait
squid	**kalamari** usually transparent, but sometimes tinged with brown. Eight short tentacles and two long. Slender body with broad fins at the tail. Flying squid **thrapsalo** are much larger with long bodies (light violet in colour) and narrow fins at the tail. Both are common and inexpensive
whiting	**backaliáros** rather a tasteless fish, common and cheap. Greyish olive-green with pale yellow to green underside

The Butcher's Shop   **Kreopoleion** Κρεοπολιον
The Butcher   **Hasapis** Χασαπησ

Sadly the quality of the meat *kreas* and butchering is not amongst the many glories of Greece. Although some meat is imported (legs of lamb, fillet steak) the rest is locally bred. Beef rarely exists although old 'cow meat' sometimes passes as such. Veal is an adequate substitute, as they are slaughtered somewhat larger than their British counterparts.

beef	**moschari** the best beef in Greece is usually imported and therefore expensive and not generally available outside Athens – so beware of old cow or oxen! Best cuts are **bon filet** fillet steak and **filetto** rump steak
chicken	**cotoppoulo** usually sold whole and dressed ready for roasting. Excellent value as more often than not free range
eggs	**avga** usually good, fresh and inexpensive
goat	**katsiki**
kid	**katsikaki** good eating and fairly common especially around Easter. Sold whole or cut like lamb
kidneys	**nephro** either lamb or pork, both plentiful and cheap. Very good. Eat on the day of purchase
lamb	**arni** the climate of Greece suits sheep and goats well, so their meat is found all over. Baby lamb is a spring delicacy and found roasted whole in many villages on feast days. When it is butchered, other than **souvlakia** (cut up in pieces ready for grilling on a skewer), the cuts are: **boutti** leg **païdakia** chops **brisolis** chump chops **stethos** breast
liver	**sicoti** common all over Greece. Either calves' or pigs'. Best eaten the same day

mince	**keyma** the mince in Greece is either ready minced (so there is no knowing what it contains) or you can ask for a piece to be minced specially. Usually it is roughly cut and is better if put through the mincer twice. Always eat within 24 hours
pork	**heirino** pork is usually a good buy in Greece although more expensive than lamb. It is sold all over the mainland but is sometimes difficult to buy in the islands. Apart from the usual **Souvlakia** pieces for grilling on skewers the cuts of pork are limited to:
	butti heirino leg of pork
	païdakia chops
	filetto fillet (rare)
	stethos heirino belly of pork
quail	**oretikia**
veal	**mosharaki** veal is quite common in Greece, particularly in the north. Strictly speaking it is young beef. The leaner cuts are excellent minced for stuffing tomatoes or aubergines. When butchered properly, the cuts include:
	filet fillet steak (when sliced it is called **schnitzel**)
	païdakia loin chops
	brisolis best end of neck cutlets
	sverco neck
	plati shoulder
	stethos breast
	butti leg

Charcuterie **Allantika**

There are plenty of pigs in Greece and consequently good by-products. The *allantika* is either part of the butcher or a shop on its own.

bacon	**bacon** not produced locally although imported can be bought prepacked, but is expensive

ham	**zambon**
mortadella	**mortadella** locally produced Italian sausage that resembles spam in appearance (only). Sold in slices but charged by weight
salami	**salami** excellent locally and nationally produced salamis compare favourably with any in Italy. Sold sliced or whole and charged by weight
sausages	**lukanika**
	horiatika lukanika a particularly fine spiced sausage

The Dairy   **Galaktopoleion** Γαλακτοπολεον

Apart from the fine cheeses and excellent yoghurt, dairy products are scarce, as most of Greece is too arid for milk cows.

butter	**vootiro** sold in ½ kilo slabs. It's unkind but accurate to say that it is usually rancid. Imported brands are available at a price
cheese	**tiri** not surprisingly, most cheese is either ewes' or goats' milk. A good rule is to stick to the local cheese – *fetta*
	fetta medium soft goats' milk cheese – very common and inexpensive
	casserie a dull, uninteresting plastic yellow cheese
	graviera similar to *Emmental* without the holes. Found mostly on the islands
	misethra ewes' milk cheese
	Danish blue commonly imported – should be blue (yellow is a sign that it is off)
cream	**crema** only found in Athens, and then with difficulty
margarine	**margarini** some imported – best of the local brands is **Beetam**

milk	**ghalla** fresh cows' milk is rare in the majority of Greek towns and villages although Long-Life milk is often available. In the sparser regions or islands goats' milk is sold, but should be boiled before use. Very often tinned milk or condensed milk is sold; it tends to be rather sweet
rice pudding	**rizogolo** delicious creamy rice pudding with cinnamon on top
yoghurt	**yaourti** made from sheeps' milk **provio**, or from goats' milk **ageladino**. One of the true delights of Greece, it is thick, creamy, wholesome and cheap. Produced everywhere it is always fresh. **Faye** (thick) and **Velouté** are good brands.

The General Store Pantopoleion Παντοπολειον
The Supermarket Supermarket

Every village has a store that positively bulges with every conceivable item: the floor strewn with open sacks of dried beans, the counter laden with pots of olives and yoghurt, shelves crammed with bottles of wine, tins and jars, hardware' and some minor medicines right up to the ceiling where frying pans and salamis hang from the beams. It is usually run by a whole family who live on the premises. The store seems to be open all day and every day (except Sundays) from 8 in the morning until 1 o'clock in the afternoon, closed during lunch and the hot afternoon, opening again at 4 o'clock in the winter, 5 in summer, until late. 'Late' can be anything from half past 7 to 10 or 11 at night.

Unlike other shops and restaurants in Greece the shop keeper will serve his customer, rather than self-service.

Modern Greek has not evolved much as a language so many things that came in during the last century or so have English names – like baking powder.

Groceries

beans, dried	**fasolia** sold out of sacks or already packed in plastic bags. The same name goes for all types of beans

beans, white	**aspra fasolia**
chick peas	**fasolia mavromatica** sold out of sacks
cinnamon	**canella** sold loose in sticks or in jars powdered
cloves	**gharifalo** sold loose or packaged in boxes
coffee	**café** as all imported, coffee in all forms is expensive
coffee, Byzantine	**vyzantino** formerly Turkish coffee though should never be referred to as that!
flour	**alevri**
flour, maize	**arithani**
honey	**meli**
jam	**marmalada**
lentils	**fackes** sold loose or prepacked, these small red or grey seeds usually still have their skins. Pick over them thoroughly before soaking as may be full of tiny stones
mayonnaise	**mayonaisa** better to make yourself, as imported is expensive and local second rate
mustard	**mustarda** local varieties are neither hot nor expensive
nutmeg	**moschokarido** commonly used in Greek confectionery and puddings
oil, olive	**eleolado** usually only one quality and is expensive. It should have a fresh smell, be clear and dark green in colour
oil, vegetable	**aravosetelaio**
olives	**elies**
pasta	**macaronia** this is really spaghetti. Sizes are numbered (lower the number thicker the strands) No. 6 the best size. All other pasta has the same names as in Italian (see page 143)
pastry	**filo** a puff pastry sold ready-made in strips
pepper	**piperies**
rice	**rizi** mostly long-grained yellow rice. Ask for **rizi yah pilaf** for pilafs or **rizi yar soupa** for soups

rigani	**rigani** small leaf herb usually sold dried
salt	**allati**
sugar	**zachari**
tea	**tsai** the tea sold in Greece is somewhat inferior but herbal teas are good, particularly camomile
tomato purée	**domatopoltos**
toothpicks	**odoutoglifides**
vanilla	**vanilia** sold as essence in bottles or powdered
vinegar	**exeethi** most types available as imported – local wine vinegar good

The Baker's Shop (in a town) **Artopolion** Αρτοπολειον
The Bakery (in a village) **Fournos**

The *fournos* is 'the place of the oven' *forno*. There is at least one in every village, however small, and sometimes more as the Greeks are passionately fond of bread *psomi*. There is nothing to compare with freshly baked bread bought still warm early in the morning.

Every loaf is exactly a kilo in weight, so bread is sold by the piece. As it is so cheap it is not worth halving, although the baker will cut a loaf if asked. Only the shape alters – round, oblong or square; loaves are either white *aspro* or brown *sitazenio*. Brown is less common. The baker will expect you to test his bread for freshness, but as he bakes every day (except Sunday when villagers cook their lunches in his oven) there should be no need.

Also made and sold in the *fornari* are sweet crumbly biscuits like shortbread called *coulouria*.

Around Easter, an important time in the Greek calendar, two special shortbreads are made:

half moons	**courabeithes** sprinkled with sugar
	melomacarantha brown sticky moist shortbread, with nuts and honey

These are available in the larger cafés all year round. Any bread that has not been sold is cut up into slices and made into rusks *paximathia*.

Also sold in the *fornari* is yeast *maya*.

Baclava

Cataiffi

Kourabiedes

Galatobourreco

Samiko

Shamali

Cakes

The Cake Shop/Café **To Zacharoplastio**
Ζαχαραπλοστιο

There is no village in the whole of Greece that does not have at least one *zacharoplastio* – a place that sells wonderful sticky cakes and biscuits, all kinds of drinks, alcohol and Byzantine coffee, to eat and drink there while talking or playing *tric trac* backgammon, or to take away. It is the best, and sometimes the only place, to buy cakes and biscuits. Wines and spirits will be cheaper at the general store.

baclava	**baclava** one of the best Greek specialities of flaky pastry, honey and nuts. A recipe to make your own is on page 201
biscuits	**biscotta** there are endless varieties of biscuits in Greece as each region has its own special recipe. They are soft and sweet, sometimes with chocolate or nuts
	kourabiedes small white sugared biscuits
	voutimata 'dipping biscuits' – small biscuits served with coffee, usually with an almond on top

brioche	**brioche** common for breakfast. At Easter baked with a chocolate Easter egg inside
cake	**cake** usually a sponge cake with confectioner's cream. Often sold in slices
cataiffi	**cataiffi** a very sweet Greek speciality that looks like Shredded Wheat, drenched with honey and filled with walnuts
cream cakes	**pasta** usually a sticky cake filled with cream, also the name for the 'cake of the day'
éclairs	**éclairs** chou pastry with chocolate on top filled with confectioner's cream
ice cream	**pagoto** either made on the premises or a proprietary brand. Either vanilla **vanilia** or chocolate **chocolata**
milk cake	**galactobourico** rather a good mixture of flaky pastry with a cream

The Greengrocer's Shop **Oporopoleion**
Οποροπολειον
The Greengrocer **Manavi**

Despite her ever-increasing tourist trade Greece is virtually self-sufficient in fruit and vegetables. Consequently very little is imported, so usually only that which is in season is sold in the shops and markets.

There is little order in the hotch potch of fruit and vegetables piled on market stalls or spilling from sacks and boxes but it is all fresh and generally inexpensive.

Vegetables	**Horta**
artichokes	**anginares** globe shaped with tough, green overlapping leaves. A short spring season as the summers are too hot for it
aubergines or egg plant	**melitzanes** sometimes like a white egg, hence the name, but more often large, pendulous and deep purple

basil	**vasilicos** often used in Greek cookery although outside the larger markets with herb stalls it is difficult to find. Best to make friends with a Greek who will 'procure' some for you
bay leaves	**daphni** again difficult to find fresh it is better to get from a friendly Greek
beans, broad	**fasolia** cheap and plentiful in the spring, drying up in summer
beans, french	**fasolakia** quite plentiful throughout the summer and not expensive
beetroot	**kokinogoulia** only sold in the winter; the tops are boiled like spinach and served cold as a vegetable with vinaigrette (page 203)
cabbage	**lachano** usually the hard white salad cabbage is sold in the spring and autumn, the summers being too hot and dry
carrots	**carrota** winter vegetables
cauliflower	**counoupithi** usually much larger than British variety and not that expensive
celery	**silinon**
cucumber	**agouri** only found in the winter and spring
courgettes	**colokithakia** plentiful in summer and inexpensive, this baby marrow is dark green in colour and often sold with its orange flower
dandelion leaves	**horta** the green leaves of this common weed are widely used in Greece in salads. They are boiled first then eaten cold with vinaigrette
garlic	**scortho** plentiful and cheap they are sold by the string, *scortha*, or by the piece, *scortho*. Said to ward off the evil eye; any expression of admiration must be followed by '*scortha*' to ward off the evil eye!
leeks	**prasa**
lettuce	**maruli** dozens of varieties in winter and spring

marjoram	**manzurana** excellent herb with small leaves and tiny flowers; expensive and hard to find fresh although sold dried in the general store
marrow	**colokithi** as courgettes are so popular marrows are rarely allowed to reach maturity
mint	**diosmos** a common Greek herb more often found dried than fresh
mushrooms	**manitaria** not common outside the major towns
okra	**bamies** also known as ladies' fingers, they are light green in colour, a thin tapering octagon in shape, cheap and plentiful throughout the summer
onions	**cremethia** usually the large varieties are sold throughout the year
	cremethiakia a smaller but stronger variety
parsley	**mainthanos** large serrated leaf with a long stalk. Much used in Greek cookery and available all year round
peas	**bizellia**
peppers	**pepperíes** usually the fresh green peppers are sold. Also the hotter dried red peppers are sold in 'strings'
potatoes	**patates**
rosemary	**dendrolivano** very common herb widely used (sometimes abused) in Greek cookery, it has a strong flavour even when dried
sage	**faskomilia** usually sold dried for herb tea but occasionally found fresh
spinach	**spanaki** a common vegetable and cheap, it has dark green leaves and fleshy white edible stalks
tomatoes	**domates** a seemingly unending supply all summer, they are large, full red and particularly good for stuffing
vine leaves	**fila apo staphilia** usually given away they are used for wrapping up *dolmathes* or quail

Fruit	**Frutta**
almonds	**amithghala** available all year round, the fresh green almonds in the spring are an expensive delicacy
apples	**mila** plentiful in summer they are mostly soft eating apples like Golden Delicious
apricots	**vericocca** cheap and plentiful all summer
cherries	**kerrasia**
chestnuts	**castana** popular around Christmas
figs	**seeka** either green, red or purple they are cheap and plentiful all summer and autumn
grapes	**staphilia** good and cheap all summer and autumn
grapefruit	**grapefruit** all imported and scarce outside Athens
lemons	**lemonia** cheap and plentiful most of the year
loquats or medlars	**musmulla** delicious orange-skinned fruit sometimes with brown blotches, the succulent yellow/orange flesh has two or three large pips. Cheap and plentiful with a long season of May to autumn
melon	**peponi** either green or yellow honeydew, or the round ogden melon. Good value all through the summer
melon, water	**carpuzi** very common and so cheap that although they are usually very large they are not worth cutting up. Available all summer they have dark green skins, red flesh and jet black seeds
oranges	**portachelia** good and plentiful all summer. Either thin-skinned blood oranges, *sanguini*, or the thicker-skinned and rather sweeter *merlin*. Both are good eating, although *sanguini* are better for squeezing
peaches	**rothakino** so cheap that they can be bought by the crate, they are plentiful all summer

pears	**achlathi** either green or brown they are available most of the summer. Sometimes they are sold unripe: check by pressing the stalk end – it should give slightly
plums	**damaskina** plentiful and cheap all through the summer, the deep purple skin should have a definite bloom
strawberries	**fraoules** expensive and only available in spring and early summer
walnuts	**karithia** sold from the autumn onwards. Expensive

Wines and Spirits

The ancient Greeks worshipped Dionysus, the god of wine. Today the god is immortalized in stone and paintings, while his wine rates only as good but unexceptional – especially when compared with that of other countries.

Retsina

It is certainly worth persevering with the ubiquitous retsina as this wine is very much an acquired taste. The resin flavour is a hangover from the days when wine was stored in goatskins and sealed with pitch pine. The resin tainted the wine but gave the Greeks a liking for the flavour, which they satisfy today by adding resin artificially.

Retsina is very cheap. Usually it is white (or rather a golden colour) but there is a red *kokkino* and a rosé *kokkinelli*. To ward off a hangover the Greeks sometimes mix mineral water with their retsina!

Bottled wines
Every region has its own wine, cheap and plentiful. Bottled wines
from other regions are sold in the general store and the café. The
variety of wines depends on the size of the town or village.

Carras mainland white or red wine; good but a little expensive
Castel Danielis a good red wine but tends to be expensive
Crete: King Minos (not surprisingly) is the best known wine from
    Crete. Golden in colour, it is a pleasing wine and should be
    served chilled. *Kritika* is very dark red and powerful,
    reminiscent of the Minotaur!
Domestica undoubtedly the best known Greek wine. Either red or
    white, it is good and inexpensive
Mantinea a good white wine from the Peloponnese found all over
    Greece. Serve chilled
Nauossis Boutari a powerful red wine but very drinkable
Rhodes a prolific wine-growing island much influenced by the
    Italian occupation. *Chevalier di Rhodi* is a good example of a
    Rhodes red wine – full-bodied and not expensive
Santorini best known for Communion wines, Santorini produces
    strong red wines with a curious taste which comes from the
    rich volcanic soils

Spirits
Ouzo: distilled from grapes (usually pressings), *ouzo* is the most
common drink in the Greek cafés. It has a strong aniseed flavour
and, like retsina, is an acquired taste. The Greeks drink it straight
but it is more palatable (and less strong) if diluted with an equal
quantity of water. There are many proprietary brands and price is
usually a fair indication of quality. *Raki* is a stronger version of *ouzo*
found in *tavernas* in the islands. There are several adequate brandies in Greece and as in France, stars indicate the quality. *Metaxas*
is a good brand name.

COOKING

Plato (427–347 BC) when asked what book he was reading,
astounded his inquisitor by replying that it was the work of his
fellow philosopher Philoxemus on cooking! Sadly, despite this
pre-Christian start, Greek cuisine is rarely praised apart from the

simplest of dishes. There are plenty of fine dishes – some of which are included in this section – that are either forgotten about or are poorly prepared and served stone cold in the *tavernas*. The basic skills, the recipes and the raw materials are all there, but sadly only a minute proportion of Greeks make the most of them in their homes and in their restaurants. But there is no reason why you should not eat superbly, making the most of the local ingredients.

Avgolemono saltsa   Egg and lemon sauce

A typical sauce from Greece used with many fish, meat and vegetable dishes.

30 g/1 oz butter
2 tablespoons flour
300 ml/¹/₂ pint stock

2 eggs
juice of 2 lemons

Melt the butter in a heavy pan and add the flour. Allow to cook for a few minutes until golden – not brown. Add the stock gently stirring all the time until it is fairly stiff. Remove from the heat and allow to cool slightly. Meanwhile beat the eggs until they are frothy and add the lemon juice. Stir the egg mixture into the sauce and return to a very low heat, stirring all the time. Do not let the sauce boil or it will curdle. Season with pepper and salt.

Soupa avgolemono   Egg and lemon soup

This hot soup is particularly good and typically Greek. Serves 6.

1¹/₂ litres/3 pints stock (chicken is
best, although veal or fish are
also good)

200 g/4 oz rice
3 eggs
juice of 2 lemons

Bring the strained stock to the boil. Add the rice and simmer.

Beat the eggs with the lemon juice and a tablespoon of cold water until frothy. Scoop off a cupful of the hot stock and add it to the egg mixture, stirring slowly all the time. Repeat two or three times.

Remove rice and stock mixture from the heat, first making sure the rice is cooked, and stir in the egg mixture. Do not return to the heat as this could curdle the soup.

Serve at once.

Horta salata   Dandelion leaf salad

Dandelion leaves are so popular in Greece that they are cultivated like lettuce.

Allow 4 stems per person. Cut off roots. Wash each leaf separately. Cook in boiling salted water for 10 minutes or until tender. Drain well, then serve with olive oil and lemon dressing.

Vrouva (a yellow weed like our mustard) is also eaten a great deal in Greece. Prepare and serve like dandelion leaves. Spinach (*spanaki*) can also be prepared in the same way.

Tzatziki   Yoghurt salad

The fresh taste and excellence of Greek yoghurt makes this a particularly appetizing dish. Serves 4.

500 g/1 lb cucumber
1 pot yoghurt around 350 g/14 oz
1 tablespoon olive oil
juice of ¹/₂ lemon

Peel the cucumber and slice thinly or grate. Salt liberally and leave covered for about 1 hour.

Drain off water and squeeze cucumber dry. Mix with the yoghurt, oil and lemon juice. Season with pepper.

Chill before serving.

This makes a good cold soup if just diluted with cold water – about 1 litre/2 pints for this quantity.

Taramasalata   Smoked roe pâté

Taramasalata can be bought ready-made but is just as easy to make oneself! Serves 4.

125 g/5 oz tarama (cleaned and smoked cod or grey mullet roe, bought from the general store)
juice of 2 lemons
1 rusk paximathia *from the bakery* fornari
1 tablespoon chopped parsley
1 boiled potato
500 ml/generous ¹/₂ pint olive oil
black olives

Soak the *tarama* in cold water for a few minutes to remove some of the salt, then break the tarama into a bowl, add the lemon juice and fork over, mixing the two into a paste.

Soak the rusk in water until soft. Squeeze dry and mix with the tarama paste. Stir in chopped parsley.

Crumble the boiled potato and mix in so that the whole is now a creamy paste.

Add the oil very slowly, as if making mayonnaise, stirring in one direction only. The *tarama* will be pink in colour when it has absorbed enough oil.

Serve garnished with black olives and thin toast or rusks.

Some add a clove of crushed garlic, but I think this spoils the flavour.

Tiropitakia Cheese pasties

Filo is a special Greek pastry that can be bought in any café. It is used to 'wrap up' many delicious fillings like this recipe for tiropitakia.

8 sheets of filo *pastry (about 125 g/5 oz)*
olive oil
500 g/¹/₂ lb fetta *cheese (must not be too hard or salty)*
1 tablespoon parsley, finely chopped
2 eggs

Cut the sheets of *filo* into long strips about 6 cm/2½ in. wide and brush with oil.

Mash the cheese and parsley with a fork. Break in the two eggs and beat well together, making a thick paste.

Put a small lump of the cheese mixture on to the *filo* strip and fold over from side to side making a triangular 'envelope'.

Place all the envelopes on a greased tray and bake in a moderate oven until golden (around 15 minutes).

Serve hot or cold.

Spanakopitakia Spinach pasties

Cooked chopped spinach (about 1 kilo/2 lb) mixed with the *fetta* and made exactly the same way will use 16 sheets of *filo*.

Domates yemistes   Stuffed tomatoes

Tomatoes grow to an enormous size in Greece, and as a result there is never a menu that does not have some form of stuffed tomatoes. Serves 6.

12 large ripe tomatoes	*1 kilo/2 lb minced veal (remember*
a little sugar	*to have it minced twice by the*
8 tablespoons olive oil	*butcher)*
2 large onions	*parsley (finely chopped)*
175 g/6 oz rice	*mint (finely chopped)*
	nutmeg
	2 rusks

Cut the bottom off each tomato and remove pulp and seeds. Stand them on a baking tray adding a little sugar and salt to each.

Heat the oil in a pan and cook the onions until soft brown.

Add the rice and cook until transparent. Add the mince, herbs, nutmeg and tomato pulp. Season with salt and pepper and cook for around half hour slowly.

Meanwhile crumble the rusks and soak in a little olive oil.

Fill the tomatoes with the stuffing (leaving room for the rice to swell). Sprinkle crumbled rusks on top of the tomatoes, then a little olive oil over the tomatoes and bake in a moderate oven until tops are golden and the tomatoes wrinkled (about ½ hour).

Serve hot or cold.

Red and green peppers can be stuffed and cooked in the same way.

Dolmadakia   Stuffed vine leaves

It is the strange aromatic flavour of fresh vine leaves that gives *dolmadakia* such a unique taste. Truly Greek, they are not difficult to prepare. Serves 6.

about 50 vine leaves	*parsley (finely chopped)*
8 tablespoons olive oil	*cinnamon*
1 large onion (very finely sliced)	*100 g/4 oz rice*
1 kg/2 lb minced veal (remember to	*egg and lemon sauce (page 191)*
have it minced twice)	

Boil the vine leaves until tender and malleable. Drain.

Heat half the oil in a pan and cook the onion until soft brown. Add the remaining oil. Add the mince and 'seal' it in the pan, mixing it with the onion. Add the parsley, and season with salt, pepper and a pinch of cinnamon. Add the rice and a little water. Cook for about 5 minutes until the rice begins to swell. Allow to cool.

Take a vine leaf and roll about a dessertspoon of the stuffing up tightly, starting from the stalk end. Pack stuffed vine leaves tightly in a large saucepan and barely cover with water. Press a plate on top and cook for about 1 hour very slowly.

Make the egg and lemon sauce from the juice and pour back over the *dolmadakia.*

Serve when cool.

Bamies   Ladies' fingers (okra)

You either adore or despise okra – a typical Greek vegetable that is worth a try!

Trim the tops of the ladies' fingers, wash them thoroughly and dry. Salt them liberally and leave in the sun for about 1 hour to draw off the slime. (This is not essential but is an improvement.)

Boil in salted water for 10–15 minutes until soft.

Serve with melted butter as a vegetable, or cold with mayonnaise as a salad.

Psari lemonato yia fourno   Baked fish with lemon

A fine traditional Greek way of cooking fish, simple, with foolproof results. If the fish is oily (mackerel, amberjack or bonito), reduce the oil by half. For 4 people.

1 largish fish of any variety around 1 kg/2 lb for 4 people
juice of 1 lemon
2 tablespoons olive oil
1 onion, chopped
1 carrot, chopped

either stick celery (chopped) or ¹/₂ bulb fennel (the whispery leaves will do)
rigani *(a herb like Italian oregano)*
1 tablespoon parsley, finely chopped
1 clove garlic, finely chopped

Gut and clean the fish. Rub half the lemon juice all over it and sprinkle liberally with salt and pepper. Lay in an oven-proof dish.

Mix together remaining lemon juice, olive oil, onion, carrot, celery or fennel, *rigani*, parsley, garlic, salt and pepper, and pour over the fish. Cover with a damp cloth and leave to marinate for 1 hour in a cool place.

Bake for 45 minutes in a moderate oven, basting occasionally.

Serve hot with potatoes, or cold with a vinaigrette dressing or mayonnaise.

Psari bourdeto   Fish cooked in Corfiot style

An extremely simple recipe for cooking any of the many varieties of small to medium white fish (around 25 cm/10 in. long) like hake, whiting and grey mullet. Serves 4.

1 kg/2 lb white fish (gutted and cleaned)
1 kg/2 lb potatoes (peeled and cut into 1 inch cubes)

5 cloves garlic, finely chopped
olive oil
juice of 1 lemon
2 tablespoons parsley, chopped

Put the fish in a large casserole or heavy saucepan. Arrange the potatoes over and around the fish, add the garlic then sprinkle salt and pepper over. Pour the olive oil over the potatoes and fish, firm down and add water so that it just covers the potatoes.

Bring to the boil very slowly, then simmer gently until all the water has evaporated, leaving the oil.

Add the lemon juice and parsley and just bring it to the boil before serving from the dish.

Excellent hot but equally good cold with either mayonnaise or vinaigrette.

Barbouni   Red mullet

'Red, bearded and choice' is how the Greeks view this distinctive fish. Mullet tend to be boney, particularly the smaller ones, but the reward for separating flesh from bones is great. Serves 4.

4 large or 8 small red mullet
flour
6 tablespoons olive oil

juice of a lemon and equal quantity of white wine
a little vinegar

Wash and gut the fish, but leave the heads on and the livers in. Shake dry and roll in flour seasoned with salt and pepper.

Heat the olive oil to smoking point and fry the red mullet quickly turning once. Remove when crisp (about 2–3 minutes on each side) and drain.

Keeping the pan hot, sprinkle in as much flour as the oil will take up and stir. Allow to cook for 1 minute.

Shake together lemon juice, white wine, and dash of vinegar and pour over the flour, stirring it in over the heat. When smooth and bubbling pour over the red mullet and serve hot.

Octapothi me krassi   Octopus cooked in red wine

Undeniably this recipe entails a lot of hard work, but no cookery book that covers the Mediterranean should be without guidance for cooking octopus. I think this Greek recipe is the best; it serves 4 people.

1 octopus around 1 kg/2 lb
300 ml/¹/₂ pt olive oil
1 tablespoon tomato purée
bay leaf
1 kg/2 lb shallots (small onions will do)

1 tablespoon tomato purée
3 cloves garlic
2 glasses red wine
1 kg/2 lb potatoes

Prepare the octopus (page 14). Remove ink sac. Cut the octopus into pieces not more than 7 cm/3 ins. across. Heat the octopus very gently without any liquid to draw off its juices. This takes about 15 minutes. Shake the pan to stop it burning.

When 'sweated' add the olive oil, bay leaf, onions, tomato purée and garlic. Stir so the octopus is evenly coated with the oil and cook for a few minutes. Sprinkle with salt and pepper.

Add the contents of the ink sacs, the wine and enough water to cover the contents. Bring nearly to the boil, then simmer for 1 hour.

Add the potatoes and cook for a further ½ hour. Check that there is always enough water and wine.

Serve in soup plates with fresh bread.

Garithes vrastes   Boiled prawns

Prawns are a useful addition to any fish dish but their delicate flavour also makes them a speciality in their own right. This method of preparing them captures that flavour. Allow 300 g/12 oz per person.

Wash the prawns two or three times (each time in fresh water) to remove any sand or grit. Shake dry. Put the prawns into a pan, without any liquid, cover and heat gently. The prawns will simmer in their own juices. Shake the pan occasionally. Ten minutes should be long enough.

Allow the prawns to cool in the pan before peeling them.

Serve with mayonnaise or lemon or both.

Zargana · Garfish

A common, inexpensive fish in Greece – good eating. Its bones are a bright copper-green colour – don't be put off! They are best grilled (page 12). Allow 250 g/8 oz per person.

Moussaka

Surely the best known Greek dish. It is worthy of the time taken to prepare it. Serves 6.

1¹/₂ kg/3¹/₂ lb aubergines (the pendulous purple variety)
4 tablespoons olive oil
1 onion, finely chopped
1 kg/2 lb minced meat (preferably veal)
2 medium tomatoes, chopped

1 tablespoon parsley, chopped
1 glass red wine
1 litre/1¹/₂ pints béchamel sauce (page 204)
50 g/2 oz hard grated cheese (kefalotiri)
3 eggs

Cut up the aubergines in thin slices, salt liberally and leave to sweat for an hour. Dry on a paper towel. Heat 2 tablespoons of the oil in a pan and fry aubergines until browned on both sides. Remove and throw away the oil (it will be bitter after the aubergines).

Heat the remaining oil and cook the onion until soft brown. Add the mince, tomatoes and parsley. Stir together and add the wine – use a touch more if the mixture is still too dry. Cook slowly for 20 minutes.

Make the béchamel sauce.

Remove the meat mixture from the heat and stir in 2 tablespoons béchamel sauce.

Oil an oven dish or deep baking dish. Fill with alternate layers of aubergine and mince, starting with the aubergine, sprinkling a little grated cheese on each layer (leaving enough for the top), and finishing with aubergine.

Beat the eggs, stir them into the béchamel sauce and pour it over the dish.

Sprinkle with what is left of the grated cheese and bake for ¾ hour in a fairly hot oven until the top is a ruddy gold.

Serve hot from the dish on its own or with a salad.

Pastitsio   Macaroni with minced meat

This is a classical Greek dish even though it is identical to the recipe for Italian *lasagne* (page 158). Greece was the earlier civilization!

Follow the *lasagne* recipe, but: substitute the macaroni for the *lasagne*; use *kefalotiri* instead of *grana* cheese; use powdered milk if fresh is not available.

Kotopita   Chicken pie

Where would Greek cuisine be without *filo*? This excellent chicken pie is good hot or cold. The quantities can be doubled to provide a good cold lunch – but make sure you have a large enough dish before you start! Serves 4.

1 medium chicken, dressed	*3 eggs*
1 onion, peeled and quartered	*2 tablespoons grated cheese (use*
100 g/4 oz butter	*kefalotiri)*
3 tablespoons flour	*350 g/12 oz* filo *(about 20 sheets)*

Put the chicken in a saucepan, cover with cold salted water and bring to the boil. Add the onion and pepper. Remove white scum as it appears. Simmer gently until the flesh begins to leave the bone. Allow to cool in the broth. Pull flesh to pieces with your fingers, discarding the skin and gristle.

Melt most of the butter in a saucepan and add the flour. Allow to cool for a minute then pour in the chicken broth very slowly, stirring into the flour.

Beat the eggs with the cheese, pour into the sauce and mix well.

Add the chicken and mix together. Season to taste.

Spread half the *filo* in a baking tin, building up the layers and painting each layer with melted butter.

Spread the chicken filling evenly.

Cover with the remaining layers of *filo*, again buttering each slice. Firm round the edges, finally brushing the top with butter. Score the top into squares with a hot sharp knife.

Cover with greaseproof paper and bake in a moderate oven for 45 minutes or until golden.

Oretikia   Quail

Quail on the continent are not the expensive luxury they are in England as they are bred in huge quantities. This is one intriguing way of cooking them. Allow two or three per person.

Make a mud 'dough' of red earth and water.
    Encase the dressed quail in the mud and cook in a moderate oven until the mud is dry.
    Break open the case and the quail will be cooked.

Quails are also excellent grilled on a barbecue (page 13), but marinate them in olive oil and *rigani* for ½ an hour first.

Arni souvla   Grilled pork on a skewer

The best and most common way of cooking pork (or any other meat) anywhere from Greece to the Far East. Allow about 250 g/½ lb for a skewer, which will serve one person, so these quantities are for 4.

1 kg/2 lb lean pork	*juice of ¹/₂ lemon*
12 bay leaves	rigani
2 tablespoons olive oil	*1 lemon, quartered*

Cut the meat, if not bought cut *souvlakia*, into 5 cm/2 in. cubes. Leaving about 2 cm/1 in. at each end, thread each piece of meat on to the skewers separating them occasionally with a bay leaf.
    Shake the oil, lemon juice, *rigani*, and salt and pepper together and pour over the meat. Leave marinating for ½ to 1 hour.
    Grill on an open fire (page 13), turning often.
    Eat hot (cooling tends to toughen the meat) with lemon juice and a green tomato or yoghurt salad.

Arni psito   Roast lamb

As lamb is the best meat in Greece I am including this straight-forward recipe for roast lamb. If your oven will not take a whole leg, take it down to the village oven (*to forno*) in your baking dish, like all the locals. Serves 6.

3 cloves garlic	*4 tablespoons olive oil*
1 leg of lamb,	*juice of 1 lemon*
1¹/₂–2 kg/3¹/₂–4¹/₂ lb	*rosemary*
6 large potatoes	rigani

Cut the garlic into slithers (about 3 per clove). With the point of a sharp knife pierce the lamb all over and slip in the garlic. Place in a large baking tray.

Shake up 2 tablespoons olive oil, juice of ½ the lemon, pepper, salt and not too much rosemary, and rub mixture over the joint. Peel the potatoes, then halve and arrange round the joint. Mix the rest of the olive oil, lemon juice, *rigani*, salt, pepper and ½ litre/1 pint water. Pour mixture over the potatoes.

Cook in a moderately hot oven for 45 minutes per kilo (20 minutes per lb).

The potatoes should be brown, having absorbed the oil and water. The lamb should be pink.

Serve with a green or tomato salad.

Baclavas

A rich dessert for all Greeks and those with a *very* sweet tooth! The sale of sheets of *filo* in every café certainly widens the scope of holiday cooking, and *filo* keeps well in the refrigerator. As it is not a quick recipe, I have given larger quantities in the hope it will last longer.

1 tablespoon powdered cinnamon	syrup
350 g/12 oz chopped walnuts	*1 jar 500 g/1 lb clear honey*
500 g/1 lb butter	*225 g/8 oz sugar*
25–30 sheets filo pastry	*juice of a lemon*

Mix the cinnamon and walnuts.

Melt butter. Pour a little in a baking tin or similar and line it with 3 or 4 sheets of filo, painting each sheet with butter.

Mix half the butter with the chopped walnuts and cinnamon and spread a thin layer over the pastry. Spread another 2 sheets over this, painting with butter. Add another thin layer of the nut mixture and cover with 2 buttered sheets of filo. Continue until all the mixture is used up and you have 8–10 sheets left.

Lay the remaining sheets on top, singly, painting each one with melted butter.

Cut the top 4 layers with a sharp knife dipped in boiling water in any geometric pattern – diamonds are traditional.

Sprinkle the top with a little cold water and bake in a moderate oven until golden in colour.

While the pastry is cooking make the syrup by boiling rapidly the honey, sugar and lemon juice with about 450 ml/1 pint of water. When the mixture starts to become syrupy remove from the heat and allow to cool slightly before pouring over the cooked pastry. Allow to cool then cut up into individual portions.

Sauces and Dressings

Mayonnaise

Mayonnaise is not difficult to make, although it is hard work. Home-made mayonnaise is vastly superior to even the best of the bought varieties. Although olive oil is never really cheap in Europe it is much more expensive at home, so indulge yourself! The flavour of the oil comes through strongly, so don't use too strong-tasting an oil.

2 egg yolks
1/2 tablespoon made-up mustard (or
 1/2 teaspoon mustard powder)

1/2 litre/3/4 pint olive oil
juice of 1/2 a lemon

Make sure that all the utensils are absolutely clean and dry.

Put the egg yolks (make sure there is no white) into a bowl with the mustard, pepper and salt. Stir hard until creamy. While still stirring, add the olive oil at first drop by drop so that the mixture takes up the oil. After you have added half the oil, pour the rest in gradually in a thin stream, stirring hard all the time. You will see when the mixture can take the rest.

If the mixture curdles (separates into egg strings in the oil), start again with another egg yolk. Add the curdled mixture to the yolk as if it were the oil.

The sauce should have a firm consistency, almost like a soft jelly. When all the oil has been taken up add the lemon juice and stir a final time.

A good way to cheat making mayonnaise is to add a tablespoon of bought mayonnaise to the egg yolks. Some leave the yolks for an hour to solidify a little before starting.

Vinaigrette

Vinaigrette is essential to all salads. It keeps well so I suggest that you make up a larger quantity and keep it in a screw-top bottle.

to make about ¾ litre

3 wineglasses olive oil
1 wineglass tarragon or wine vinegar
1 clove of garlic, sliced into 3

1 teaspoon mustard powder, or 3 teaspoons made-up mustard
pinch of sugar

Put all the ingredients into a bowl and whisk until the oil and vinegar are thoroughly amalgamated.

If you prefer a less acid dressing, use rather less vinegar. Another variation is to use lemon juice instead of vinegar.

Béchamel sauce

The world owes a great deal to Louis de Béchamel, Louis X I V's chef, who invented this sauce.

50 g/2 oz butter
50 g/2 oz flour
¹/₂ litre/1³/₄ pint milk

Melt the butter in a saucepan, sprinkle in the flour and stir with a wooden spoon. Allow to cook on a low heat for a few minutes until golden.

Take off the heat and add all the milk. Stir well.

Return to the heat, stirring constantly until the mixture thickens. Season with salt and plenty of black pepper.

Index of Recipes

Index of Principal Ingredients